Don't Just Deal

Going From Surviving to Thriving When Everything
Changes

DIANA CARTER

DEDICATION

For my husband, Tyler. You are my most cherished blessing and my favorite unexpected change. The greatest joy of my little life is just living it by your side. I love you more.

TABLE OF CONTENTS

"Just deal with it."

It sounds kind of harsh, right? Like maybe I'm telling you to pick yourself up by your bootstraps (do people really have bootstraps anymore?) and move on with your life - regardless of what's going on or what you may be facing. Like I don't care about the details and just want you to get over it.

Right?

I mean - when I hear the phrase, "Deal with it," I picture a conversation that lacks compassion and sensitivity and where one person simply refuses to try and see things from the other person's perspective.

Can you picture it? Have you been there?

Maybe it was a breakup.
Maybe it was not getting that job you interviewed for.
Maybe it was a move to a new city, graduating from college or getting engaged.

You were sharing your heart with a friend - sitting there verbally processing the jolt that some sort of change brought to your life – and whoever you were talking to looked at you and said, "Just deal with it."

My response? "Mmmmm, thanks, friend." (With only a little more than a slight bit of sarcasm and sass.)

Hear this: That's not the heart of this book. This is not a 30-day journey to self-improvement, mental toughness or emotional intelligence. This is not a book written with hopes of helping you become better at "dealing with it." While none of those things are inherently bad things - I just don't see any of them as the main thing.

So, what can you expect? What is the main thing?

In the pages that follow, you'll find 30-days of brief devotionals aimed to help you gracefully walk through life's changes and transitions. Together, we'll walk through the different kinds of change, why change rattles us, some of the constant realities we can park our minds on when change comes - and so much more. The goal? To help you do more than just deal with it - to take you from surviving to thriving when you encounter change.

You can do the devotionals on a Monday through Friday schedule over the course of six-weeks or you can go straight through for 30-days. Heck - you can even read it straight through in one sitting if you want. You can do them when you wake up in the morning, before you go to bed at night or on your lunch break.

Honestly - you can approach this book however you'd like. I have just one request: Answer the questions. Write down your answers and maybe even your prayers too.

Each devo contains three parts:

— The actual devotional content - a quick look at how God's at work in the midst of every change
— Kick Around Questions - questions to help you dig a little deeper into God's truth
— Prayer Nudge - a related prayer prompt "nudging" you into a two-way conversation with God

Go get yourself a journal. It doesn't have to be anything fancy! It can be a $0.99 marble notebook from the dollar store - which happen to be this girl's favorite.

Just take the time to write out your answers (to the Kick Around Questions for each day) and your prayers (in response to each day's little Prayer Nudge).

Recording where you are - right here and right now, in this very season - is such a gift to future you. More than that - it's such a tangible way to see God's hand at work when you're on the other side of "change" and reading through your own words.

My sincerest prayer is that this devotional would play only a small part in the way the Lord is transforming you in all areas of your life.

You are His, boo. And I cannot wait for you to see that truth hold up in the midst of life's changes.

Less without beauties like you,

Diana Carter
Founder, Because I'm His

An Introduction to Change

DAY 1
WHAT IS CHANGE?

C hange. It's one of life's constants – something that we can come to expect as we grow, age, live, breathe, get comfortable, least expect it, etc.

We can never outrun it, escape it or avoid it. It's everywhere. We read quotes about change, books about change (like this one!), listen to talks about change and even take courses on topics like "change management."

Sometimes we choose change and sometimes change chooses us. Sometimes change is good and sometimes change seems anything but that.

But there's one thing change always has in common: it's uncomfortable. Even the most exciting and anticipated of changes bring about some level of discomfort. For most of us – the very thought of change even possibly floating into our tranquil horizon makes us want to scrap the rose water facial toner and just crawl right out of our skin.

The newness of it – of change or a transition – can knock you out like a nasty stomach flu. And getting back on your feet can sometimes look like letting it run its course and resting in its effects.

For many reasons – a number of which we will dive into together over the next 30 days – change is uncomfortable.

We are a people – a generation – who is conditioned to hate change.

We hashtag #dontleavemesummer because we hate when seasons change.

We boycott Facebook after platform updates because we hate when our muscle memory has to change.

We resist things like thick eyebrows and white sneakers because we hate when fashion trends change.

We criticize John Mayer's new album because we hate when someone's sound changes.

We hate buying the next dress size up because we hate when our bodies change.

We cry after haircuts, stay in dead-end jobs, date the guy we know is wrong for us and cling to the way things were – all because we hate change.

We even pay for things in dimes and nickels because we hate carrying around change. (Anyone else?)

But why? Why do we hate change so dang much?

Is it because we thrive on control? Is it because change challenges us to go with the flow when we'd much rather know what to expect?

Maybe. I think that's all part of it. I really do.

Beneath the wanderlust and the hunger for new things, new places and new experiences is our fundamental need for safety and security. We like to know where we stand and what's expected of us. We like to know that needs will be met, bills will be paid, feelings will be acknowledged (and perhaps reciprocated) and that we will always have a place at the table. And when anything threatens this solidified position – whether in a relationship, a community, a job or an internal feeling of self-acceptance – the red flag goes up.

Even the most free-spirited of us crave some sort of permanence.

We want to know we matter – that our preferences, our opinions, our routines and our needs are all validated. And when change comes and sweeps life as we know it up into its gust? It's sometimes hard to feel like we have a place in it all. Sometimes, change makes us question where and if we really belong.

We'll celebrate a colleague's promotion, but cringe at thinking of her replacement. We'll Instagram, "Congrats to these two love birds!" when our roommate gets engaged, but no sooner than the first like pops up, we immediately begin to panic as we wonder how we'll afford the rent. We count down the days until graduation for our entire senior year, but then when we're in the home stretch, the pit in our stomach grows as we wonder, "What's next?" We spend months or years trying to get pregnant and then the second that pee-stick has a red plus sign, we question if we're really cut out for motherhood.

Change has a way of unraveling us. It has a way of sneaking into the most solid foundations of our soul and pricking little pinholes in our confidence and beliefs. It does something to each of us that – sometimes – brings out the ugly and suddenly, we find ourselves kicking and screaming, face-first on the floor.

(Oh. You've never had an episode like that? Sit tight, sister. We'll get there. Trust me.)

Over the next few days, we'll dive into the different types of change together – but for now, let's end here, reflecting on the inescapable reality of change and how it's intersected with our lives.

The grass withers, the flower fades, but the word of our God will stand forever.

Isaiah 40:8 (ESV)

KICK AROUND QUESTIONS

1) What was the biggest life change (good or bad) you ever experienced? What made it so huge?

2) Looking back on that change now, can you see actual change – or did things kind of, sort of stay the same?

PRAYER NUDGE
(Pro Tip: When I journal my prayers, I write them as if they're letters to God and start with, "Dear God…")

Ask God to show you areas of your life where you're afraid of change. Ask Him to reveal whatever it is you're clinging onto to and then when He does, ask Him to help you hold that thing / person / comfort, etc. with open hands.

You can be as real, raw and honest with Him as you need to be. Trust me, it's worth it.

DAY 2
WHEN YOU'VE CHANGED

I've gone up one — if not two — pant sizes since my wedding day in May 2016. If I'm being honest, I'm not entirely sure I would even be able to zip up my wedding dress if I tried it on right now. In fact, I went from not being able to fit into my clothes because they were falling off of me in the months leading up to our wedding (because of stress), to not being able to fit into my clothes because they don't fit over my hips almost two years later.

For most of my life, I've been the tall and skinny girl. At 5'11", my weight never really caught up to my height. And while many of you are probably rolling your eyes going, "And I'm supposed to feel bad for you?" let me let you in on a little secret and tell you that being the tall, noodly kid isn't as glamorous as it may seem. (You always want what you can't have, right?)

My identity was — at least in part — wrapped up in my status as an athlete. *Diana Carter? She's that really tall and really skinny girl who runs a lot.* So, when the description changed, I had a hard time feeling like myself. Even though – in some way – I was in control of that change (e.g., my decision to cut back on running), it didn't feel good.

You see, the world likes to tell us that our identity is something we create; that life is like a choose-your-own-adventure novel when it comes to who we are, where we end up and what we deserve.

We live in a well-meaning society where phrases like, "Work hard and you'll succeed," or "Make good choices and you'll have a good life," are spoken over us since the day we're born. We are quick to identify ourselves as So-And-So's girlfriend or the youngest member of the Executive Committee — and we have a tendency to place more value on how cute we look in the tunic we got from the pop-up sale than how deeply we're rooted in the truth of who God says we are.

Culture tells us that identities can change; that we can reinvent ourselves after breakups, setbacks or major moves across the country. But what culture forgets to tell us is this:

True identity is both fixed and absolute. True identity is not made, but deemed. True identity does not change.

We can be wives and friends and teachers and entrepreneurs, but none of those things are permanent. We can be the anxious one or the funny one or the skinny one or the pretty one, but none of those things are lasting. We can have wealth, health, influence and happiness, but none of those things carry eternal weight.

And all of those things? They can change overnight.

Relationship statuses change.
Jobs change.
Feelings change.
Bodies change.
Health changes.
Finances change.

It's all shifting sand. It's all at risk of being washed away as life's tides come in and out.

But as God's creation, we are loved by Him. Without reservation, without hesitation and without revocation, we are extravagantly loved by God. This is the only thing that will never ever change.

This is the truest thing about us. This is our *real* identity.

Yet continually, we (this girl included!) look for our worth in things and accolades and job titles and pant sizes. I misplace my identity multiple times a day — and if I'm not careful and if I wade in the detour too much — it can affect my attitude toward others and toward God.

I'll look in the mirror and all but curse the way my skin stretches over my bones. I'll question my beauty or my worth or my value based-off a bi-weekly weigh-in. I'll try on six pairs of shorts that definitely do not fit and I'll tear up as I fold them back into my drawer.

It makes sense doesn't it? The way we feel empty and disappointed when our misplaced identities change. When we put all of our eggs in a basket that was never meant to define us, we're quickly reminded of our need for Christ's resurrection to do the defining.

The solution is as straight-forward as it is hard to execute — let the position we have in Christ define us.

This means being content in who we are because of Whose we are.

This means knowing that our size and weight and relationship status and job and health all may change — but our worth will never waver.

This means establishing our value as purchased daughters of the King and never forgetting the depths to which Jesus went just to give us that title.

Culture won't tell you that you're worth anything unless you make a name for yourself. But Jesus? He thinks you're to die for just the way you are.

See what kind of love the Father has given to us, that we should be called children of God; and so we are.

1 John 3:1 (ESV)

KICK AROUND QUESTIONS

1) Name one way you've changed over the past two years. Has that change been hard for you? Are you happy with it or have you experienced some grief over it? Has it been hard for you to accept?

2) Have you ever wrestled with identifying yourself based on something worldly? Has there been something in your life that used to identify you, but doesn't anymore? (This thing that identified you can be good or bad!)

PRAYER NUDGE

Shoot straight with your Maker, girl.

Talk to God about ways you've misidentified yourself in the past. Maybe it's been by your physical appearance, maybe it's been by your status, or maybe it's been by what you've achieved. Ask Him how He wants you to think of yourself; how He wants you to see yourself and how He wants to shape your identity.

Write down the words or phrases He reveals to you and check to see if they align with what He says about you in the Bible. (Pro Tip: You can Google phrases like, "What does God say about me being beautiful?" or "Does God really think I am righteous?" and do some digging!)

DAY 3
WHEN THEY'VE CHANGED

When I was 10-years old, my baby sister, Emma, was born. With fiery red hair and a crinkled face, Emma burst into this world on a cold day in March 1999.

But.... before we continue, let's air out some dirty laundry. (My mom loves to tell this story about me – so if you haven't already heard it, here's your opportunity to hear it from the horse's mouth...)

When I found out my mom was pregnant with Emma, I was nine years old. My older sister, Faith, was 12 and we'd gone the entirety of our childhood thinking it would just be the two of us forever. Faith would beg for another sibling – but I was perfectly content as the baby.

I loved being doted on. I loved the attention. I loved being cared for and carried and slept with and fed. It was as if the birth order gods looked down upon me and said, "You were created for this. And this is where you'll stay."

And then, one day, my baby-being-glory was over.

Faith and I went to my grandparents' house after school because my mom "wasn't feeling well" and my dad went with her to the doctor. When they came to pick us up, they walked into the wallpapered living room and sat us down on my grandma's couch. I knew something was up.

"We're having a little baby!" my mom said, a hesitant smile plastered across her face as she waited to see how we would react.

Faith, of course, angel-child in all her ways, responded exactly how you might expect the responsible oldest sibling to respond. She instantly lit up and beamed as she jumped up and down with pure, unbridled excitement.

Me?

Well, my mom likes to say I didn't even bend my legs and just threw myself to the ground. In complete shock, my knees locked and I fell forward to the floor.

Tim-berrrrrrr!

There I stayed as I quite literally kicked and screamed the words, "No! You promised I was the baby," over and over again.

I know. A picture of a completely normal child, right? (Love you, Em!)

Flash forward nine months and my posture toward Baby Emma couldn't have been any different. Really, once my mom started to show, I began to get excited about the idea of a little baby joining our family. Now, some 19-years later, and those who know me know that Baby Emma hung the moon in my eyes and, to me, she can do no wrong. She's my little buddy and is still one of my favorite surprises to this day.

But here's the thing – babies? They don't keep.

Baby Emma is now 19-years old. She is a total babe of a young woman with a personality that fills the room and a heart that's big enough to house the orphans of the world. I couldn't be prouder of the woman she's become and is becoming.

It seems as though overnight my sweet Baby Emma transformed into the woman I catch myself daydreaming about being. And as proud as I am of her – this change has been hard.

You see, when Emma was three or four – I was who she wanted. Sure, she wanted my mom and dad like any other kid, but when her and I were home together? She wanted nothing more than to play with me and to be the center of my attention. We played games with laundry baskets and plastic horses. We'd go for walks around the block and beg my mom and dad to take us to the park. We'd make up dance routines to the likes of Adele and Austin Mahone, film them and then spend hours laughing at how ridiculous we looked.

We were buddies. And in many ways – we still are.

But life happens, right? And we grow up and, often times, relationships change. Like those creases that appear in the corner of our eyes and across our foreheads – suddenly, over time our relationships can look a little bit different.

Emma is still my little buddy, she is. But these days, instead of hiding under laundry baskets and filming music videos – we talk about work. And friendships. And our parents. And life.

Instead of sleeping under the same roof and bickering over fresh fruit at breakfast, I sleep in my house with my husband, Tyler, and she sleeps in her room at my parents' house.

Instead of me babysitting her when my parents go out to dinner, I ask her out to dinner.

I'd like to say that I saw this coming – the whole, "my little sister will eventually not be little anymore," but in many ways, this change caught me off-guard.

When people change without consulting us (as they often do), we feel a little like we've been left behind. We don't just mourn the absence of who they were – but we grieve the way life was when they were that person too.

Maybe you've experienced this in some way or another.

Maybe it was your younger sibling, too, or maybe it was a boyfriend or a spouse or a best friend or someone you looked up to who – over time – changed. Maybe one morning you woke up and, without even knowing it, that was the last day things would be "how they always were" with that person.

"People change," is what other people say when you process this certain type of grief out loud. When you lament over the loss and cling to the way things were – other people tell you to get up and move on. Yet – deep inside – somewhere, somehow, your heart craves a relationship with Someone who will never change. Someone so reliable that you can love and relate and lean in with reckless abandon.

Hang tight, sister. We're going there – and we'll get there together.

Put not your trust in princes, in a son of man, in whom there is no salvation.

Psalm 146:3 (ESV)

KICK AROUND QUESTIONS

1. Is there someone in your life whose change (good or bad) was hard for you to deal with? If yes, how did this person change and what about the change was so hard to process?

2. Why do you think we struggle to accept when people around us change for the worse? What about when they change for the better?

PRAYER NUDGE

Identify one person in your life who is going through a negative change right now. Pray for this person and ask God to reveal Himself to him / her in a way that is so tangible, they cannot deny it. Ask God to give you wisdom on how you can come alongside this person in love and show them your support.

DAY 4
WHEN IT CHANGED

I n the first year or two after graduating college, I remember saying the phrase below at least three thousand times:

I feel like I'm in middle school again.

I felt unsettled in my new stage. Like a baby giraffe wobbling as it tries to walk on its long noodle-like legs, I felt visibly unstable as I mapped out step after unstable step.

My best friends no longer lived 6 feet from me. I stopped running into familiar faces as I walked across the quad or found a seat in the dining hall because I was 700 miles away from the quad and the dining hall. The regular rhythm of class and workouts and dinners and Sunday night homework sessions were gone.

For four years, everything revolved around that place and the schedules it dictated. And to take it one step further, all of my "people" had that common ground to revolve around too. It was almost as if we lived in this little bubble – our own little sliver of the real world that connected us in ways so deep that our basis for community felt knit into our angsty hearts.

College has a way of doing that, doesn't it? Not in a negative way by any means – but it corrals us into this ecosystem that is a microcosm of the world on the other side of the stage. We have student governments, social hierarchies, campus police, responsibilities, etc. – and all of it falls under the umbrella of our pursuit of higher education.

And then – on one hot and sticky mid-morning in May 2011 – it all stopped.

After the confetti was swept up and all of the photos of me in a black cap and gown were posted to Facebook, I was suddenly navigating the new terrain of alleged stability found in post-grad life. Gone were the days of summer vacations and packing up to head back to school in the fall. The routine I'd practiced for seventeen years changed as I walked across the stage in the muggy convocation center of my small liberal arts college.

As I floundered my way through the post-grad life, I found small snippets of comfortable rhythms; little flickers or hope amidst the instability.

Things like the community of Jesus followers I'd cozied up to. The friends from work who were starting to feel like my real-life brothers and sisters. The coffee shops I frequented. The small apartment I made my own.

But as a whole, I still found myself with a huge chunk of that unsettled, unstable and "what the mess am I doing?" tucked away in the back of my head. It almost felt that as time went on, I began to feel more and more unsettled. Like, maybe the word "unsettled" didn't even begin to cover it.

For a long laundry list of reasons, my footing appeared to be fumbling.

And sisters? I'm a fixer. Oh, heavens to Betsy – I am a fixer.

And when I am unsettled? When things aren't quite figured out? When every detail isn't set in stone? I become fixated on fixing. I cannot sleep, cannot eat and cannot sit still until I have it figured out. Until my ducks are in a row, I become a slave to settling the aftermath of the rumbles.

Despite the fact that things looked fairly settled on the outside – job, apartment, friends, etc. – I felt so incredibly jostled on the inside. In the most dramatic sense of the word, I kind of felt like everything I ever knew was ripped from my white knuckles. Even though I saw it coming, even though I knew graduation was up ahead – for whatever reason, I never quite had as firm of a grasp on how it would actually play out in my life.

So for a good bit – I was sad. Like really, really sad.

I can remember calling my college roommate, at this point living in Charleston, South Carolina, from my parents' house in New York. I would call her and cry and tell her how much I missed her, how I felt like everybody I saw on Facebook and Instagram hadn't skipped a beat since the "glory days" of college and I was home with my parents, lonely and in a job that wasn't my dream one.

I can remember browsing LinkedIn and seeing people from my graduating class with job titles like "Vice President of Sales," or "Director of Marketing," and feeling like my "Account Specialist" role somehow made me inferior or less than.

I can remember watching friend after doggone friend get engaged to their college boyfriend and think, "When will it be my turn? When will my life *really* start?"

Out of sheer desperation, I found myself turning to Jesus in ways I never had before. Instead of just praying for the energy and clarity needed to pass exams or write papers – I was suddenly praying for His all-consuming joy as I went to work a job I didn't exactly love. Instead of being intentional about balancing time between by girlfriends and my boyfriend – I was suddenly being intentional about asking God for friends in my hometown. Instead of focusing on other peoples' lives and achievements – I asked God for the courage to step into whatever He wanted for me, in the very place He had me.

He was faithful, as He always is. And slowly but surely, He taught me that when our circumstances change, our perspectives often need to change too. When the change is inevitable and out of our control, sometimes the urge to resist it backs us in a corner of bitterness, negativity, self-loathing and defeat. But when we look to Jesus in spite of our changing circumstances and we ask Him to change our hearts, our hearts have a propensity to come around just in the nick of time.

Trust in the LORD with all your heart, and do not lean on your own understanding. In all your ways acknowledge Him, and He will make straight your paths.

Proverbs 3:5-6 (ESV)

KICK AROUND QUESTIONS

1. When things change circumstantially in your life (e.g., your favorite restaurant closes, your best friend moves away, you graduate or start a new job, etc.), how do you generally react? Do you see a fresh start or are you more prone to living in the past?

2. Identify a change you are going through presently. Do you need to ask God to change your heart toward whatever is happening and to shift your focus to Him?

PRAYER NUDGE

Ask God to show you ways you can root yourself deeper in the permanence of His truth. Ask Him to change your perspective toward change and to enable you to lean into Him when things are uncertain, instead of clinging to what was.

DAY 5
WHEN WE LONG FOR CHANGE

We talked about this a little bit yesterday – but in the spirit of transparency, I'm just going to come right out and say it: For a while I was one of those girls who was OBSESSED with getting married.

Yes. Me. I was that girl.

You know the one who slips, "When we get married," into every conversation about her and her boyfriend? The one with the Pinterest boards and the guest list already saved to her laptop?

Yes. That was me.

During my sophomore year of college, I started dating a guy who I would end up dating for five years. If you're a superstar mathlete, you've figured out that it means we dated until we were almost three years out of college. What you might not be able to figure out from your arithmetic is that we went to a small liberal arts college that was also a Christian college.

And yes – what they say about those kinds of schools is true, girl.

Ring before Spring!
"I'm here for my MRS degree."
Engaged (and sometimes married) before graduation.

All of it. It's true. At least, it was for me and our small little school tucked away in the foothills of North Carolina's piedmont region.

By our junior year, my boyfriend and I found ourselves in a friend group of six couples. One of those couples got married before our senior year and four more were engaged within a year of graduation. Again, for the mathletes, this means that by about two years post-grad, we were the only couple out of that friend group that hadn't taken an official step toward marriage. While everyone else was husband and wife or fiancé and fiancée, we were still just boyfriend and girlfriend.

Sure, we talked about it – because I always brought it up, remember? But there was no ring. There were no plans. And, later, I learned there was never really any intention to pursue it.

In my heart of hearts, I desired marriage.

Looking back, I can be honest with myself and acknowledge that at least part of my desire for marriage was rooted in insecurity and the insatiable need to keep up with everyone around me. Yet, to this day, I trust with all that is in me that my desire to be a wife and a mama was stitched into my heart by God Himself – and in my sinful flesh – I somehow came to corrupt its purity. I know not everyone can relate to the acute awareness of the desire for marriage, but from the age of about 19 or 20, God pretty much spoke this into my heart with a certainty and clarity that was indisputable.

I desired marriage with every last bit of my soul. I hoped for it with all that was in me.

Can you relate?

Maybe for you it isn't marriage or being a mom. Maybe it's a career or a restored relationship with a parent. Maybe it's a God-dream of starting your own nonprofit or becoming a long-term missionary.

Let's shoot straight for a second and just snip-snap cut to the chase: We all know what it's like to desperately want something. We've all had dreams about, journaled about, asked our friends about, bent God's ear about (over and over and over and over again) something.

A desire, a passion, a relationship, a goal, an internship, a job. Something.

We've all hoped for something with all of our might – and most of us have probably sat silent next to a friend as she hoped her heart straight out of her chest that her *want* would become a *have*.

We have all been there. Every last one of us.

And most of us – most of us human beings down here waddling around on this side of eternity – have spent our fair share of seconds, minutes, hours and days in a waiting room. Some of us have even spent years waiting for something.

We can wait for things – for dreams, for passions, for relationships, for goals, for desires – but we must never stop waiting for the Lord. We can hope for things – for approval, for love, for families, for jobs, for houses, for big and grand white kitchens – but we must never place our hope in anything but the Lord.

Life is not a waiting room where we sit around and count down the seconds, minutes, hours and days until our want arrives. Life is space to wait for the Lord – our Hope that is already here.

And in the waiting? We get to live and love and lean and learn.

Is it imperfect? Yes.

Are there tears and a lot of asking God why? Yes.

Have I figured it out? No.

But I know there's beauty in the process. I know that He is with me in my waiting and that in just one second, He is able to accomplish far more than I could ever dream or imagine in years of my own control-freak doing.

Wait for the LORD; be strong and let your heart take courage; wait for the LORD!

Psalm 27:14 (ESV)

KICK AROUND QUESTIONS

1. Jot down one thing you are waiting on or hoping for right now. If you've not yet prayed about this today, go ahead and take a minute to pray for this specifically.

2. Do you feel like you are hoping for whatever you wrote above - or putting your hope in whatever you wrote above? Are you able to determine the difference?

PRAYER NUDGE

Wherever you're writing your prayers, write down your answer to the first Kick Around Question above. Pretend you're talking to God face-to-face and write out what you would tell Him about your desire or hope.

Thank Him for who He is and let Him know that, no matter what, you trust Him. (If that last part isn't true for you today, be honest! Ask Him to help you trust Him in all circumstances - even in the waiting!)

Why Change Rattles Us

DAY 6
CHANGE TOYS WITH OUR COMFORT

I'm one of those people who craves being around her people.

Once you become a "safe person" to me (e.g., Tyler, my best friends, vulnerable coworkers, etc.), you pretty much become a secondary form of comfort and I feel like I can take on any situation with you by my side.

So, three-ish years after college graduation, when my relationship with my boyfriend was on the rocks – I moved to Charlotte to preserve the comfort found in our bond.

In reality, I moved to Charlotte in a last-ditch effort to pour what was left of me into that disintegrating relationship. It wasn't my sole motivator – but I would be lying through my semi-straight teeth if I said that my desire to revive a relationship that was past its expiration date wasn't cresting the "Reasons I am Moving to Charlotte" list.

At the same time, the decision to pack up my deeply rooted New York life and take whatever I could carry south of the Mason-Dixon line wasn't one made in haste. In fact, it was the exact opposite.

Making the move to Charlotte was something that I prayed about and sought Godly counsel on for close to a year – and to this day, I am indebted to those who listened to me jabber about it for all that time. It was something that, after much prayerful deliberation, I eventually trusted as a clear path set before me. So much so that the prospect of finally arriving and immediately walking into tumult and instability didn't deter me.

In fact, the very day after I gave final and irrevocable, "I'm moving to Charlotte," notice to my boss, the prophetic words, "I don't think I want to marry you, Diana," were whispered over the phone. And while the words shook me to my absolute core, I was somehow immovable in my resolution to move to Charlotte and work on a dying relationship.

Still, something in me said, "Just go." And it was a voice that even the most devastating of blows couldn't veto.

Looking back – the timing was impeccable. Had the relationship taken such a drastic turn-for-the-worst even just days earlier, I might not have ever made it to Charlotte. Had those predictive syllables been spoken any sooner, I might've missed out on everything good and life-giving that was waiting for me here. On the outside, it looked like a sign – a warning, an omen – that I should stay put in my 10 x 10 bungalow in the Long Island colonial in which I trudged through braces and AP exams and college applications. Making the move just wasn't worth the risk and I'd be much better suited to just keep on keeping on right there in New York.

But on the inside, the timing was a divine gut-check. It dimly hushed, "You said you trusted Me, right? Now, follow Me."

And so, six months later, I went.

Somehow, with a deteriorating relationship and my hope for marriage still intact, I arrived in Charlotte and was immediately welcomed with the dysfunction that comes with a spiritless connection. Gone were the days of buoyancy and joy. The relationship was lifeless – and efforts to revive its vitality were unabashedly unilateral. But still, I held on. I wrung out every last drop of idealism that churned in me and labored toward rejuvenation until one day, I gave up. In a parking lot on Independence Day (go ahead, revel in that irony!), I sat defeated in my efforts to love and to love well. I listened to five years of intertwining and consolidation come to a screeching halt and unravel in just two hours. I half-heartedly petitioned a handful of times and then I gave in. My clenched fists opened up finger by finger and finally, I let go.

It was done.

There was no shock, really.

It was like a rug had been pulled out from under me – but in a fashion that was so slow, I actually watched my feet slide clumsy across the surface – inch by inch, bit by bit – until, eventually, I was standing sockless on the cold wood floor.

So there I stood – barefoot. And my person, my comfort was gone.

I've heard it said that outside of your comfort zone is "where the magic happens," yet in those days and weeks following our breakup, life felt anything but magical.

But again, change pointed me to God as I sought to process where He'd led me and how He'd graciously brought me there.

I thought about how for the year leading up to the break, I had clenched fists, white knuckles and a stubborn-as-a-pit-bull refusal to let go of something that wasn't mine anymore.

I thought about the debilitating pain that came with realizing that certain things may've never really been yours to begin with and I thought about how when hurt people hurt people, it's just an opportunity to show mercy to a mercy-hungry world.

I thought about the ways I'd learned grace – how it's an all-around game-changer when you dive thick into the mess of it and decide you're going to let it be your lead.

I thought about how no one really talks about it, but sometimes following God can feel like falling on a rusty, jagged sword, but how that's what we are called to do.

I thought about how – ultimately – my comfort isn't wrapped in human flesh or walking around holding my hand and kissing my forehead. I thought about how comfort – true comfort – is so much more than the worldly things we put stock in.

True comfort is a person, yes. But this Person is Jesus and He is both with us and within us. And this Jesus? He never leaves us high and dry – and comfort is who He is.

As one whom his mother comforts, so I will comfort you; you shall be comforted in Jerusalem.

Isaiah 66:13 (ESV)

KICK AROUND QUESTIONS

1. Where are some of the places you turn to for comfort? List out as many as you can name.

2. Do you struggle with turning to God for comfort first? If yes, why? If not, what are some tips you would give someone who does?

PRAYER NUDGE

Ask God to be your comfort – in times of change, in times of despair and in times of exhaustion. Ask His presence to be so real to you that if you close your eyes, it feels like He is right there in the flesh.

Ask Him to draw you to Himself in moments of weakness – in moments when you are in deep need of comfort. Thank Him in advance for the ways He will make good on His promise to comfort you.

DAY 7
CHANGE SHOWS US WE'RE NOT IN CONTROL

I met my sweet husband, Tyler, on a blind date in Charlotte almost a year after my college relationship ended.

After dating for a year and a half, Tyler proposed to me on Thanksgiving Day. We watched the Thanksgiving Day parade with his mom and then showered and got ready for the holiday celebrations. Before heading to his grandparents' house for dinner and games, he drove me to nearby Lake Chatuge – a beautiful lake rimmed by the Great Smoky Mountains. He held my hand as we walked over to the spillway, got down on one knee and asked me to be his wife. It was the same exact spot where his dad proposed to his mom some 30-years earlier and everything about the way he asked was sincere, romantic and positively perfect.

We knew we wanted a relatively short engagement, so we set the date for May 20th and gave ourselves six months to prepare for our big day. About halfway through our engagement we were celebrating my 27th birthday when I was confronted with how *not* in control I was.

We'd just pulled into my apartment's parking lot when I started to feel a little bit off. My heart was racing, my stomach was uneasy and I felt like I wanted to crawl out of my skin. We walked into my apartment and I excused myself upstairs to my room to change.

Before I knew it – I was having a full-fledged panic attack.

My heart now felt like it was going to thump into my throat and cause me to throw up.

I wanted to sit and stand and lay down and run a marathon all at once.

I kept fluttering between crying and not being able to produce words because I could hardly breathe.

It felt like this panic attack came out of the clear blue skies – but looking back, I can see how life really was kind of a "perfect storm" in that season.

Meticulously planning a wedding in less than six months.

Tension in my relationship with my older sister.

Preparing for marriage and trying to learn how to be a wife.

Work pressures mounting atop a crazy travel schedule and a gargantuan annual event for which I felt almost solely responsible.

In a season I'd always thought would be filled with joyous anticipation, I started to find myself filled with dread.

The anxiety I was dealing with took on a life of its own and I quickly began to spiral out of control. What I thought was an isolated incident was actually a launch pad into a 10-month battle with a diagnosed anxiety and panic disorder. Our wedding landed in month 3 of this struggle – and to this day – it hurts to admit that I felt a bit of dread on our wedding day.

Let me explain.

Despite the many clinical definitions of anxiety – mine was simply this: The mind's uncanny ability to transform any fear – no matter how far off or how irrational – into a very real and threatening reality. For me, these fears were both in the distant future and distant past – fears of what was to come and fears of who I was. It even reached a point of being as cyclical as the fear of feeling fear.

I could not reason with my anxious thoughts because they operated outside of any logic. For example, during this season, I could acknowledge, believe and know something as 100% truth and anxiety could latch onto it and coax my mind into poking holes in it. Eventually, I was tempted to believe the exact opposite of what was true.

This particular breed of anxiety didn't care about statistics or odds, it did not take the reality, facts or figures of a situation into consideration. It made its own assumptions and lived life defining its own story, its own reality.

Eventually, the constant anxiety led to regular panic attacks (like the one that happened on my birthday) that would interrupt every aspect of my life.

I would physically shake.

I would gag and feel like I was going to vomit.

I couldn't eat anything and survived on meal replacement shakes because they were the only things I could stomach.

I wasn't sleeping.

I almost always felt dizzy and like I could pass out.

I had chest pains.

I couldn't travel or be alone.

I could barely leave the house.

I began building a "safe place" for myself by cutting people off and attempting to control what I could. I told my boss I couldn't travel anymore and he graciously obliged. I would stop meeting people for lunches or dinners because I knew I wouldn't be able to eat. I begged Tyler to stay at my place as late as he could – often asking him to spend the night in the guest room.

Anxiety and panic ganged up on me and tried to convince me that more control would bring me the peace I so desperately wanted.

I listened to it.

And I isolated myself.

Two weeks before our wedding, I couldn't take it anymore. I was at what I thought was rock bottom. I was crying in my bedroom when Tyler came over. I confessed how I was dreading our wedding day because I was absolutely terrified of having a panic attack and ruining what we had both been looking forward to for a long, long time. I was so scared that I would crumble under the sheer stress and natural nerves that would present themselves on that day.

Trying to control everything (see above) wasn't working. I began to realize that feeling like I needed to control everything played a huge part in what landed me in this cycle of anxiety.

And when I didn't know how to break it and when I didn't know where to begin surrendering my "control", I began to panic even more.

You see, the illusion of control is perhaps one of the most damaging lies we are fed as Christians. Particularly Christian women. The world will tell you that having your ducks in a row and having a plan and being Type A is the preferred (or only) way to live life, but hear this:

You are not in control.

You never have been and you never will be. More control does not equate to more peace. In fact, the more we try and grab at control – the more we begin to obsess over having things figured out and neatly planned – the more opportunity the enemy has to pile stress and anxiety on our plate.

The good news? We know the One who is in control. And He is worthy of all our trust.

The heart of man plans his way, but the Lord establishes his steps.

Proverbs 16:9 (ESV)

KICK AROUND QUESTIONS

1. Do you struggle with the need to be in control? If yes, how does the need to be in control manifest itself in your life?

2. Why do you think we believe the lie that the more control we have, the more peace we will have? How can we combat that lie with truth?

PRAYER NUDGE

Chat with God about some of the ways you've clung for control in your own life. If you're feeling extra bold, as you pray, place your open hands on your lap with your palms facing up to the ceiling. Tell God, with your words and your posture, that you trust Him, that you surrender the reins to Him – and then thank Him for being the One in control.

DAY 8
CHANGE QUESTIONS OUR IDENTITY

t the root of my struggle with anxiety and panic was… an identity crisis.

In the midst of frequent panic attacks and a physiological inability to level my own emotions – I began to question everything.

Was I crazy?
Was this who I was now?
Was this who I was all along?
Was I hiding something from myself?
Would I feel like this forever?
Could I really be a good wife? A good mom?
What if I was a total failure at both?
What if I let everyone around me down?

I began to doubt everything about who I was, about the freedom I had been granted through Jesus' death and resurrection and about what God wanted to do in and with my life.

Being a wife and being married was something I wanted for as long as I could remember – and meeting and dating Tyler only intensified that desire. When it was finally on the cusp of coming to fruition, I came face-to-face with fears I had about my own inadequacy.

By God's grace, I made it through our wedding day with joy that trumped any feeling of anxiety or nervousness. Yes, I was still wrapped up in the disordered thoughts and had to stave off a couple of panic attacks – but when the red doors to the little white chapel opened up and I saw Tyler standing at the end of the aisle, my heart about leapt out of my chest.

I was shaking, yes, from the nerves of the day – but we said our vows, kissed in front of our families and friends, and then danced the night away as husband and wife. And every last bit of it was beautiful and intimate.

For about two days, I'd convinced myself that I was "better." After the wedding and for the first bit of our honeymoon, I convinced myself that I was "coming down" from all of the stress of wedding planning and that I'd be back to normal soon. That this whole episode of being taken down by my own mind was only a result of high stress – not something I'd actually have to address.

Cue the universe texting me a big "LOL, NO."

I'd long heard it said that marriage doesn't complete you or solve your problems – it does the exact opposite: exposes and intensifies your short-comings. Let me be the first to tell you that truer words have never been spoken about marriage, okay?

Tyler was so sweet in the way he loved me as anxiety and panic moved in like two additional spouses in our marriage. His patience, grace and love is what ultimately prompted me to seek Christian counseling – and he was not bothered by the hefty price tag per session, only encouraging as he said, "We will do whatever it takes to help you get better, sweetie." Lord, bless this man.

So I went to counseling. And through it – I realized that for as many times as I'd heard, "Your identity is in Christ," as a Christian – I had zero clue what that actually meant in my life. It was hard work getting to a place where that statement carried any weight – but me, the Lord and my sweet truth-speaker of a counselor put in the work.

I spent a lot of time with my nose in my Bible.

I didn't do this to be holy.
I didn't do this so I could check-off the box.
I did it as a means of survival.
I did it because God's word was truly the only thing that could bring me snippets of peace when everything around me seemed to be spinning out of control.

Sleep was a prized delicacy during this time – yet when my alarm went off each morning, I peeled back the covers without ever hitting snooze. Sleep was precious, yes, but time with God was even more cherished.

I'd pour my coffee, plop down on my couch and pull a fleece blanket up over my legs. With shaking hands, a clouded head and a knotted stomach, I'd grab my Bible and my journal and begin digging into God's word like it was my first meal after a long fast. In the beginning, even as I read truth, my mind was plagued with interruptions masked as dark and anxious thoughts.

It was as if there was a force of darkness poised against me, doing everything in its power to keep me from the life-giving fruits of God's word.

Out of pure desperation, I got more intentional. I buckled down and became more determined than ever to keep the enemy out.

I opened my journal and began to write out qualities of God in one column and then what those qualities meant for me in another column.

Because God is with me, I don't have to fear. (Isaiah 41:10)

Because God's forgiven me, I have no shame. (Isaiah 54:4)

Because God loves me, I am cared for. (1 Peter 5:7)

Because God is all powerful, I am kept safe. (Psalm 46:1)

Because I am His, I am redeemed, loved, whole, safe, forgiven, capable, more than a conqueror, free, strong and accepted.

(Just to name a few, right?)

And slowly, the more I rooted my identity in the truth of what God's word said about me, the chains of anxiety didn't seem so heavy and tight. Eventually, they stopped digging into my wrists and, unlocked, they fell right off. The deeper and more intimately aware of who God said I was, the weaker and sillier the lies the enemy slung at me started to seem.

Lies shrink, shirk and shrivel in the presence of His almighty truth.

But to all who did receive him, who believed in his name, he gave the right to become children of God.

John 1:12 (ESV)

KICK AROUND QUESTIONS

1. Do the things you believe about yourself align with how God views you and the identity He gave you? Or are you believing any lies about who you are? (If you don't know, do a quick Google search for something like, "What does the Bible say about our identity?" or "What is my identity in Christ?")

2. What is the one thing God says about you that is the hardest for you to believe about yourself? Why is this so hard for you to believe? Some examples are that you are fully loved yet fully known, forgiven, free, justified, holy, righteous, a co-heir with Christ, etc.

PRAYER NUDGE

Reflect on your answer to number two above and ask God to uproot whatever it is that is preventing you from living in the reality of who He says you are. If you struggled to answer the question, ask Him to reveal aspects of your God-given identity that are hard for you to live out. Thank Him for being the only One who could ever define you.

DAY 9
CHANGE THREATENS OUR STATUS

The road back from anxiety and panic was a long and arduous one – but, by God's grace in the form of counseling and modern medicine, I can gratefully say that I am on the other side of the battle. I can now be fully present in my marriage because I am not constantly questioning who I am or what I'm worth.

This new-found freedom led me to a big "leap of faith," fully supported by my sweet Tyler. (Are you sick of how much I brag on him yet? I'm sorry – but he really is as wonderful as I'm leading you to believe! I've said a million times that I wish every woman had a Tyler – just not mine. Okay, sorry. Gag. Back to the point...)

In May 2017, I left my job as a marketer for a Fortune 500 company to work in full-time ministry at a large multisite church here in Charlotte. I'd been at my previous company for six years and absolutely loved it. The people, the work, the leadership – everything. But it wasn't really my dream.

I went through college and the beginning of my post-grad life enamored by stories of people who wrote books while living out of the back of their car or sold everything they owned to do medical missions in Rwanda. I was captivated by the protagonist's ability to seemingly disregard cultural expectations and to build their lives on something more than the definition of success I've long been accustomed to.

There was something about their commitment to their dream – to deep, intrinsic satisfaction – that's always been so attractive to me. There was no fear of not having a hefty 401(k) balance by age 55, no regret over disappointing those who had different dreams for them, and no compulsion to justify their decision to those who maybe just didn't quite get it.

Everything about it seemed brave.

Through the years, the pull toward pursuing a calling has been further magnified by my faith and the all too harsh reality that our time on this planet is so very brief.

So one day I went for it.

I left Corporate America, took a 35% pay cut and turned over the fancy title and financial security that came with it.

I'd love to be able to say that since taking that leap – life has been all butterflies and roses – but it hasn't.

Despite me knowing with all that is in me that I am exactly where God wants me – in the exact position, in the exact church body and on the exact team within our staff – it's still challenging. Despite choosing this change and marching into it head on – there are still days when I wrestle with the what ifs.

What if I stayed at my old job? Would we be debt-free by now? Imagine the title you'd have by now… the money you'd be making…

I know full well that no one goes into ministry for the money and I also know that God has been doing more with less in mine and Tyler's lives financially since I took this job. I can stand before you and say that His provision has astounded us and that even with 35% less coming in, He's directed us toward a contentment that has spurred us to a mindset of generosity we never knew existed.

But then there's my heart, right? There's the part about this change that is still half-wrapped up in the loss of my identity as a big-time corporate marketer and half-mourning the reality that life in ministry will likely never be as glamorous as a job that sent me to Isle of Palms, Orlando, West Palm, San Francisco and Chicago – just to name a few.

Even though I chose this change – and even though I go to work every day deliriously grateful for the opportunity to devote my vocational life to God's Kingdom – if I'm honest, there's still part of me that needs God to work on my obsession with status.

Since stepping into this role, I've said the below statement (or some version of it) approximately 8,000 times:

At my old role, I felt pressure because I put it on myself. I wanted to desperately climb the corporate ladder and to make a name for myself. I wanted people to know, "Diana Carter put this together. She was the brains behind this operation and the whole thing was her idea." In ministry, I feel pressure because what I'm doing matters. This is Kingdom work.

The worst part? I think I may've convinced myself this is true.

And for the most part, it really is true. I do care deeply about my role and the quality of the work I produce at my church because it is directly tied to the advancement of God's Kingdom here on earth. But what isn't entirely true is that I've somehow stopped caring about my status.

While I'm no longer in "Rat Race" mode – I can't say that I don't care about recognition. (That sentence pains my heart to write.) It feels good to hear someone say, "Diana, great job on that presentation. You really landed the plane for us." It feels good to hear someone say, "I haven't stopped bragging about what a value you are to our team."

And I a little bit still relish in knowing I'm doing a good job. I don't necessarily think it's bad to take pride in your work – but when taking pride becomes being proud (like it so easily does for me), it can become a problem.

When I left my corporate job, I gave up a status.

I gave up the "Marketing Director" title. I gave up the goodwill equity I'd built over six years. I gave up a salary I'd watch climb year over fiscal year. I gave up wining and dining clients, the over-the-top conferences and the "need" to shop at places with dressing room attendants.

When I left, I talked a big game that I didn't value the same things the world did (i.e., money, titles, luxury, etc.), but apparently, part of me isn't so different than the world after all.

Caring about status? I think that's a part of me that will need progressive sanctification. As I work out my salvation on this side of Heaven, I pray God will remind me that when my earthly status is in jeopardy, my standing with Him is never changing.

For by the grace given to me I say to everyone among you not to think of himself more highly than he ought to think, but to think with sober judgment, each according to the measure of faith that God has assigned.

Romans 12:3 (ESV)

KICK AROUND QUESTIONS

1. Do you have an "obsession with status"? If yes, what about status is tempting for you to obsess over? If no, how have you safeguarded your heart against caring about status?

2. Have you ever experienced a change that, in effect, changed your status? If yes, what was it and how so?

PRAYER NUDGE

Get real with God and ask Him to show you ways you've cared about status without even knowing it. Ask Him to search your heart and gently convict you to show you places where you've cared more about what other people thought of you or how you were perceived than you should have. Confess this tendency to Him and ask Him to humble you with His love and to remind you that your true status is His child.

DAY 10
CHANGE USHERS IN THE UNKNOWN

S o far you know that I am…

— A has-been athlete whose body looks way different at 29 than it did at 25
— A once reluctant middle child turned proud big sister
— A girl who had a hard time adjusting after graduation
— A former marriage-idolizer
— A survivor of Generalized Anxiety and Panic Disorder
— A former corporate marketer who made the jump into ministry, yet still struggles with pride

Phew! We've covered a lot of ground in just nine days, huh? Now that you know all of my dirty little secrets that are tidied up… let me fill you in on some of the messy emotions I'm dealing with right now, okay?

I feel really, really settled. Like almost too settled.

Tyler and I are in a sweet spot in our marriage. We love our home, have the most perfect little dog, redid our backyard (on a budget!), both love our jobs and are just all around grateful.

My parents moved from New York this past November and are in their groove. Emma lives in the same city as me again and I couldn't be happier to have my little buddy with me. Faith and her husband, Joe, still live in New York with my angel of a niece, Olivia, and another little bugger on the way.

Tyler's family is close to us again and we get to see our niece and nephews on the Carter side more than we ever have before.

I've fully embraced my passion to write, teach and speak and have started mentoring a group of younger women as I seek to "be who I needed five years ago" to those just a few steps behind me.

In reality – I am in this utopian type season and I'm a little bit hesitant to get too comfortable.

Why? Because I have no idea how long it will last.

Yes. The girl writing a devotional on change is, in fact, scared of change.

I find myself wondering things like…

— When will I be a mom? What will life look like then? Will I still want to write as much? Will I even have time to think about writing? Will I enjoy work as much as I do now? What will our marriage look like when we're not just Diana and Tyler – but mom and dad?
— Will I always work in ministry? What about when my boss changes or if our leadership changes? What will that look like for me?
— Will we always live in Charlotte? If Tyler got a solid job offer somewhere else one day – would we leave?

— What about our friends? Will they always live here in Charlotte? Will we still like it if / when they leave?

I wonder about change, sometimes. What it will look like, how it will manifest itself in the here and now, when it will come and how we will react. I wonder about the big picture changes, yes. But I tend to find myself – as noted above – lost in the details of change.

It's like my obsession with the unknown is fed – over and over again – by playing out the details of what every possible unknown scenario could ever look like.

Maybe we say, "The devil is in the details," because God really isn't concerned with them in the same way we are. Maybe God has a supernatural capacity to know where He will take us, but leaves the "getting there" up to us.

Maybe God cares less about where we go, what we say and what we do, and more about how closely we follow, how deeply we love and how much we lean into Him. Maybe the most paralyzing and conniving trick the devil throws in our path is an insatiable obsession with the details.

If the devil is in the details of the unknown, let's add them to the pile of things we surrender to Jesus. If the enemy tries to preoccupy us with the how's and the why's and the when's – let's be a generation that continually turns (and returns) our eyes to the Who, amen?

He determines the number of the stars; he gives to all of them their names. Great is our Lord, and abundant in power; his understanding is beyond measure.

Psalm 147:4-5 (ESV)

KICK AROUND QUESTIONS

1. Are you someone who is intrigued by the unknown or scared of it? Why?

2. Do you find yourself spending a lot of time thinking about the "what if" type questions (like some of the ones listed above)? If yes, jot down a few of the "what ifs" you're thinking about right now.

PRAYER NUDGE

Surrender the details of the unknown over to God. Hand over the burden of the future and the outcomes to God – to the same God who determines the number of stars and knows them by name. Give Him the what if's and the maybe's. Thank Him for being trustworthy – for being a God we can relentlessly follow and know, beyond a shadow of a doubt, is on our side and working for our good.

When Change Chooses You

DAY 11
REMEMBER JOB

I f you are unfamiliar with the book of Job, I would strongly encourage you to read it in its entirety. Maybe even in one sitting. If reading 42 chapters seems like a little much for you – try The Message (paraphrase) version or try listening to The Message version. Think of it like a podcast and throw it on while you're driving or while loading the dishwasher.

Trust me – it's a doozy and you definitely don't want to miss it.

In the event you haven't read Job yet – or if you need a little refresher, here's my super succinct paraphrase of the book:

Job is a blameless and upright man in the land of Uz. He lives a pretty cush life, has ten kids, a wife and a whole bunch of sheep, camels, donkeys and oxen. The whole shebang. One of the most important things to know about Job is that he fears God, rejects evil and even prays for his kids any time they have a party – in the event one of them sinned. Think of him as an all-around good guy who loves the Lord.

One day, Satan (the accuser) approaches God and basically says that the only reason Job loves and obeys God is because God has given him a good life filled with many blessings. God disagrees (because He knows that Satan isn't right) and agrees to let Satan strip Job of everything he has in order to prove that he will still worship God in spite of the plot twist. God gives Satan one premise: Do whatever you want – just don't harm him. (Job 1:6-12)

In one single day – Job finds out that his livestock, servants and children have all died for various terrible reasons. In deep anguish, he rips off his clothes, shaves his head and mourns. (We've all been there, am I right?) In spite of the blows, Job still blesses God in his prayers of desperation.

Proved wrong, Satan returns to God and says, "Okay. You were right. But if I got him sick… if I afflicted his own body, then he would turn from you." God gives Satan the green light to test Job again (Job 2:1-6) and Job is inflicted with painful sores and ulcers all over his body. Scripture tells us that the sores are so itchy and painful that Job actually breaks a piece of pottery to scrape himself as he sat atop a pile of ashes (Job 2:8). Amidst the physical agony and anguish he experiences, we are told that Job still does not sin – even though his wife encourages him to curse God and give up on life (Job 2:9-10).

When three of Job's friends heard the suffering he was enduring, they came from faraway places to just sit and be with Job. Or, so we thought at first. In the midst of Job crying out to God and cursing the day he was born; wishing it never happened and that the very day was erased from the calendar – Job's first friend, Eliphaz, speaks out and implies that Job must not truly be innocent before the Lord if this was happening to him (Job 4:7-9). The friends and Job go back and forth and back and forth a bunch of times and Job continues to declare his innocence (which we know is true – see Job 1:1) and his friends keep insinuating that he must've sinned in order for all of these horrible things to happen to him. They even go as far as imagining the types of sin Job must've committed to warrant this sort of punishment from God.

Eventually, Job gives up on his friends and goes straight to God.

In his anguish, Job tries to come up with a conclusion for why these awful things have happened to him. He argues (with God) that it isn't fair and bounces all over the place thinking God is not just at all (and that He is the one who orchestrates evil) and that He takes pleasure in inflicting pain on us. He continues to assert his innocence, unable to understand why he deserves what has happened, and asks God to directly answer him.

A fourth, unexpected, friend shows up – Elihu (Job 32). Elihu doesn't exactly answer why Job specifically is suffering, but he reminds Job that God is good and just and proposes that God sometimes allows us to suffer to develop our character or warn us of future sin.

And then – God speaks. He responds to Job and calls *him* out for calling *Him* out. "Where were you when I laid the foundation of the earth?" God asks in Job 38:4. He goes on to remind Job that God has always been and always will be in control. He reminds Job that He sees it all, that He is the one who formed it all and that He is good and just. Then, God makes a joke – and it's the kind of joke that would make me blush at how silly I was being. He tells Job He will gladly hand over the reins; that He would be more than happy to let him take a stab at ruling the universe (Job 40:8-14).

As God continues to lay the smackdown on Job and build His case by saying, "Look… I made this place. I am just. I am good. I get to do what I want because this is My earth. This is all because of Me. I get to call the shots, regardless of if you understand why I do what I do. I didn't do this because you deserved it." In the final chapter of the book, Job repents for the way he dealt with this giant trial and humbles himself under God's goodness and authority. God turns to Job's friends (yup, they're still there!) and scorns them for the way they insinuated that Job must've deserved this life as punishment. He basically calls them out for lying to Job about His character and kicking him while he was down.

In the end, Job's losses were restored – and then doubled. God blessed Job's life and we are told he died "an old man and full of days," (Job 42:17).

Dang! That was a lot to condense into just a few paragraphs – but my prayer is you get the gist now.

Job's story is particularly rich to me for a couple reasons – but the main reason is just because it seems so real. So often I feel like I put Bible stories in this category of "happening long ago in a faraway land," and I unintentionally remove myself from the weight they carry.

But Job? I feel like I see his story played out everywhere I look. It's a story of tragedy. And it's one we are all too familiar with, amen?

We see tragedy scrolled across news headlines and Twitter feeds.

We see it plastered on crowdfunding accounts for causes like a young father's memorial fund or the desire to pursue a cancer treatment that insurance won't cover.

We see tragedy, too, in faraway places – but so often, we see it in our neighborhoods, in our schools and in our families.

Job's story is one of change that was 100% out of his control. It was a series of unfortunate changes that not only chose him but changed him.

And for the next four days, we're going to pick apart some of the ways we can learn from Job and the monumental changes he went through.

Though he slay me, I will hope in him; yet I will argue my ways to his face.

Job 13:15 (ESV)

KICK AROUND QUESTIONS

1. What is your initial reaction to Job's story? Be honest! Write down your first few thoughts.

2. Why do you think God allows Satan to target Job?

PRAYER NUDGE

Ask God to deepen your understanding of the story of Job. In the places of Job's story where you struggle to see God's goodness or fairness, ask Him to strengthen your faith. Take it a step further. In the places, situations or changes in your own life where you struggle to see God's goodness, ask Him to make His character known to you in ways He's never done before. Beg Him for the ability to see His goodness in all areas of your life.

DAY 12
IT'S OKAY TO MOURN

I know I already confessed this – but during the first few months after I graduated college, I frequently called my college roommate in tears. She was in Physical Therapy school in Charleston and still in the whole school schedule and mindset – and I had begrudgingly entered the real world. Even though she'd moved on from undergrad like me, I still envied her close connection to the lifestyle I'd grown accustomed to over the previous four years.

I'd call her and cry because I missed her – but deep down, I also cried because I was mourning the loss of everything I knew.

College was pretty great for me. I don't say this in a prideful or haughty way at all, but from the moment I arrived on campus, I had friends. Because I was an athlete, I kind of had this built-in friend group that (whether I liked it or not) became my default community. In addition to track and cross country, I was involved in our campus ministry team and Fellowship of Christian Athletes. I connected well with the people in my classes and I worked hard to cultivate relationships with girls on my hall and, later, in my apartment complex. Outside of all of those environments, I had a solid group of friends that made all of the moments in between class, practice and sleeping memorable.

When I walked across the stage in the convocation center in May 2011, a part of me felt like I watched the life I spent four years building fade into the distance.

A week after graduation, I packed all I could into my two-door Honda Civic and made the drive from Charlotte to Long Island. Each mile marker that passed was another mile between me and the life I loved for four whole years.

When I finally got home to New York – I had a blast. Well, at least I made the people on the internet think I was having a blast. These were the days before Instagram and SnapChat – but I still made every effort to broadcast my highlight reel across Facebook, Twitter and my blog. In part, I really do think that I thought I was enjoying life.

I loved living home with my mom, dad and two sisters. Looking back, those last couple of years when we all lived in our little colonial together (before weddings and babies) hold some of our family's sweetest memories. I also loved being smackdab in the middle of New York City and the ocean – a place that's always ushered in feelings of comfort, familiarity and home.

But in reality, I think a part of me refused to acknowledge the fact that I wasn't all that happy in my post-grad life. I think a part of me felt guilty for letting the "on top of the world" feeling fade after I walked across that stage at graduation. I think another part of me felt like every other person I graduated with was living their best life, loving their first job and smoothly transitioning out of college while I just… floundered.

And all of those parts? They didn't leave me feeling very whole.

For a long time after college, I didn't want to look back and miss it. I didn't want to be one of those people who looked so forward to something, only to be utterly disappointed when it arrived.

But there I was. That was me. And the worst part about it was that I felt like I was the only one feeling this way. Like I was the only one not having the time of my life, the only one missing the "good ol'days."

Because of this, I refused to believe that God could allow me to mourn. I refused to see grieving as a normal part of change; an essential part that exists to draw us closer to Him.

You see, I think God gives us permission to mourn. More than that – I think He kind of expects us to and delights at the opportunity to turn our mourning into joy. He knows we're human, He knows we're emotional beings, He knows we are resistant to change – and because of all that, I think He knows certain things will lead us to mourning.

Just look at Job.

When God allowed Satan to tempt Job, He did so with ultimate authority. He (God) was in control the entire time – He was calling the shots even though He'd turned over Job's possessions and health to Satan. God knew Job and He knew Job well (Job 1:8). He knew Job's tendencies and his heart. He knew what was dear to him.

When Satan robbed Job of his wealth? Of his sons? Of his status? God knew Job would mourn – but He also knew that he wouldn't turn from righteousness. (See Job 1:21-22)

Throughout the course of Job's life – we see him mourn hard. We see him literally curse the day he was born and wish it off the calendar (Job 3). We see him question the possibility of ever bouncing back – we see him hold nothing back as he verbally processes this anguish before the Lord (Job 7:11).

Yet – even in Job's mourning – we see a deep trust and a sincere worship emerge.

In chapter 13, we see one of the most famous Bible verses uttered from the lips of a mourning Job. Verse 15 reads, "Though He slay me, I will hope in Him, yet I will argue my ways to His face." We see a similar sentiment in chapter 19 verse 25, "For I know that my Redeemer lives, and at the last He will stand upon the earth."

Job's freedom in mourning leads him to freedom in praise. And God longs for us to walk the same path when we find ourselves in seasons of change.

Give yourself permission to mourn, sister. He already has – and He's waiting to walk alongside you as you journey into the most vulnerable kind of worship you will ever experience.

Blessed are those who mourn, for they shall be comforted.

Matthew 5:4 (ESV)

KICK AROUND QUESTIONS

1. Is there something in your life that you need to allow yourself to mourn? Is there a particular season that's come to a close that you need to grieve? (It's not, "No big deal." If something hurts – if you feel this tension in your soul – let yourself mourn.)

2. Do you naturally feel the freedom to mourn certain changes in your life? Why or why not?

PRAYER NUDGE

Give your grief to God. What does this mean? Tell Him why you're grieving and lay it all on the line. As you work through the mourning, ask God to give you the same freedom in mourning that Job experienced. And then praise Him. Praise Him. Praise God for being a good God who never changes – even as we mourn.

DAY 13
IT'S OKAY TO WRESTLE

When things fell apart a few months after I moved to Charlotte, God and I did a lot of wrestling. Even though I knew God wanted me here– even though I knew I wasn't here by mistake, I wasn't quite sure why He would've brought me here under such unpleasant circumstances.

Where I was hopeful for a proposal and a revived relationship – God was leading me toward singleness.

Where I was looking forward to things going "back to normal" once I settled in my new apartment – God was leading me and my boyfriend farther and farther apart.

Where I was expectant and a little bit naive – God was whispering, "I got this, D. It's not going to feel great for a bit, but I've got you. I promise."

And so I leaned into it all – the breakup, the singleness and all of the awkward conversation with new friends asking, "When will we get to meet your boyfriend?" I leaned in partly because I had no choice, but partly because I'd seen God work before and I knew better than to try and stand in His way.

I'd be lying if I told you it was easy. I'd be doing you a total disservice if I didn't tell you that I have journals upon tear-stained journals filled with prayers for a reconciled relationship; questions about God's motive, intentions and plan; and confessions of anger and disappointment.

For months – I wrestled with why God had led me out into this "wilderness" of pain in Charlotte when I was perfectly content to stay in the relational murk back in New York. Basically, I was the Israelites on the edges of the Red Sea (see Exodus 14) and God was about to show up big in my life in Charlotte.

But not before I wrestled some more.

Like Job, I'd grown accustomed to some of the comforts this life – and particularly this relationship – afforded me. We talked about this in Day 6 – but this person had (rather unhealthily) become my stand-in for God. When I was stressed, I called him. When I was scared, I called him. When I was overwhelmed, disappointed, frustrated, confused, embarrassed, etc., I called him. And I wasn't just calling him to vent or to let out some steam – but I was calling him so he could fix it.

Looking back, I can see how this was not in God's design. He never intended another human or any earthly thing to replace our dependence on Him. But in that season, I felt abandoned. I felt alone. And I felt humiliated.

I'd picked up everything and left my life in New York in hopes of repairing a broken relationship, remember? Against the better judgments of those who loved me, I would repeatedly say, "Once we're in the same city again, things will be better. Things will go back to normal." And when they didn't? I felt like Job in chapter 12, verse 4.

When all of this comfort was pried from my hands, like Job, I struggled to reconcile God's goodness with what was happening. I spent my mornings force-feeding myself the character of God and my nights in fervent prayer for this relationship to be restored. For sins to be forgiven on both ends and for the Holy Spirit to bind our hearts together – as I always thought He would. I even enlisted the most fervent prayer warriors I knew to bend God's ear on behalf of this love.

In chapter 30, Job is talking straight to God (in that unbridled, hold-nothing-back way) and he says, "I cry to you for help and you do not answer me; I stand, and you only look at me," (Job 30:20).

I am going to shoot straight with you here and say: This is exactly how I felt.

I prayed and prayed and prayed for our relationship to be repaired, for this breakup to be only a part of our love story – for it to be the part we look back on and say, "God brought us there, but then He brought us here – to this altar, in front of all of our family and friends. To this covenant union of marriage." But it wasn't happening.

The restoration wasn't on its way. At least not in the way I pleaded with God to provide it.

As you've pieced together by now – the boyfriend I dated in college was not Tyler. I did not end up marrying that man and I did not see restoration or reconciliation. Forgiveness has long been granted on my end, and I have asked God for that same forgiveness for the things I did wrong – but there was no closure or tying everything up in a neat little bow after the dust had settled.

For a good bit of time – this was hard. I waited for it to come long after I "moved on" and accepted the fact that this love was, in fact, over. I took God back to the mat and wrestled through this reality too.

Didn't He want reconciliation for us? Even if it meant not dating again?

Didn't He want His sons and daughters to be at peace?

Wasn't I called to be a peacemaker, wherever possible?

I didn't understand why God would allow things to end in such brokenness between two believers. I didn't understand how He would allow this hurt, this betrayal to linger without wrapping it up nicely.

Where was the lesson?
Where was the theme?
Where was the ending?

I talked to God about this over and over and over again – ad nauseum. More tears. More journals. More late-night prayers.

But maybe that's the point of wrestling, right? Maybe the whole point of being in the ring with God isn't for either one of us to pin the other down and say, "Ha! I told you so!" Maybe we've missed the mark here. Maybe the whole point of wrestling is the nearness it cultivates – between us and our Creator. Maybe the whole reason He even allows us to be led to the ring is to bring us closer to His heart than we'd ever get without the change.

Draw near to God, and he will draw near to you. Cleanse your hands, you sinners, and purify your hearts, you double-minded.

James 4:8 (ESV)

KICK AROUND QUESTIONS

1. Look up Job 30:20. Have you ever felt like Job did in this passage? Write about it below.

2. Do you struggle allowing yourself to wrestle with God? Do you agree with the above in that wrestling with God is a healthy way to draw near to Him? Or do you think it's wrong to interact with God in this way?

PRAYER NUDGE

Think of a change in your life that you haven't particularly enjoyed. Consider ways you've questioned God's plan in the midst of this change – and wrestle it out on paper. Be as honest as you can with God about what you're feeling. Share the good, bad and the ugly with Him. Be real and raw and don't feel any pressure to use flowery language or formalities. Shoot straight with God – this page is your ring.

DAY 14
IT'S NOT ALL PUNISHMENT

Job's whole issue with God was simple: He didn't understand what he did to deserve the disaster that his life had become.

"Teach me and I will be silent," he says in chapter 6 verse 24. "Make me understand how I have gone astray."

As far as Job was concerned, he wasn't a likely candidate for this sort of tragedy. In Job 6:10, he proclaims, "I have not denied the words of the Holy One."

Job simply cannot reconcile the punishment he is enduring – the same punishment his friends are saying he must've had coming. Some friends, right?

Job (and his friends) operated under the premise of Deuteronomic Theology. Deuteronomic Theology is just a fancy way of saying this: When we are obedient, God blesses us. When we are not obedient – or when we sin – God punishes us.

This theme is prevalent in several books of the Old Testament (Proverbs and most of the prophetic books) but is largely challenged through Job and his story.

If Job was considered "blameless and upright" by God Himself (Job 1:8), then why was he enduring such terrible calamities? If God explicitly states that Job flees from evil, then why would He punish him?

These are some of the questions Job is getting at in his conversations with his friends. He continually states his innocence and wrestles with the idea that he is being wrongfully punished by God.

He wrestles because he is human. Because he is in pain. Because he cannot understand what the mess is going on in his life. He simply cannot accept that he did something to deserve this.

Yesterday, we talked about how we do this too. We talked about how God invites us to wrestle and relishes in the intimacy it breeds between us and Him.

And as we wrestle, I think we need to fight hard against the Deuteronomic Theology embedded in our culture and in our hearts. I think we need to call out the voices in our head that whisper lies like, "You had this coming," or "Why would God bless someone like you anyway?"

Of course, many of our actions have direct natural consequences, right?

If we are unfaithful to a spouse, our marriage eventually suffers.

If we do not honor our bodies as temples of God by taking care of them, our health eventually suffers.

If we do not apply ourselves at work or in school, our careers / grades eventually suffer.

But when change comes our way for no reason – when we get the diagnosis or we lose the baby or our company downsizes or our dreams don't come to fruition – we can't default to thinking God is punishing us for some unconfessed or unforgiven sin.

Just as Job pushed up against the notion that he must've done something to deserve such tragedy to enter his life, we must do the same.

Because Jesus bore God's wrath for our sin – once and for all – we don't have to live under fear of being condemned for our sins (Romans 8:1). You may know Romans 8:1, "Therefore, there is now no condemnation for those who are in Christ Jesus," but what you may not know is the Greek word for condemnation. The word used in this verse is κατάκριμα (katakrima) and it literally means penalty.

We know that there is no eternal penalty for us because we are covered under God's grace – but we can also rest in knowing that any sort of hardship that enters our lives on this side of eternity it not God's angry punishment but His deep Fatherly *love* for us.

I get it. I get it. I know.

Now you're thinking, "But, Diana… you mean that even the bad and awful things in my life are coming from a place of love from God?"

Sister – I am called to speak the truth and I believe with all my heart that, yes, that is the God-honest, Biblical truth.

I want to leave you with a passage from Hebrews 12:4-11 today. It's in The Message version below, but I would encourage you to take a look at it in whatever version is most comfortable to you.

In this all-out match against sin, others have suffered far worse than you, to say nothing of what Jesus went through—all that bloodshed! So don't feel sorry for yourselves. Or have you forgotten how good parents treat children, and that God regards you as his children?
My dear child, don't shrug off God's discipline,
     but don't be crushed by it either.
It's the child he loves that he disciplines;
     the child he embraces, he also corrects.

God is educating you; that's why you must never drop out. He's treating you as dear children. This trouble you're in isn't punishment; it's training, the normal experience of children. Only irresponsible parents leave children to fend for themselves. Would you prefer an irresponsible God? We respect our own parents for training and not spoiling us, so why not embrace God's training so we can truly live? While we were children, our parents did what seemed best to them. But God is doing what is best for us, training us to live God's holy best. At the time, discipline isn't much fun. It always feels like it's going against the grain. Later, of course, it pays off handsomely, for it's the well-trained who find themselves mature in their relationship with God. (Hebrews 12:4-11 [MSG])

There is therefore now no condemnation for those who are in Christ Jesus.

Romans 8:1 (ESV)

KICK AROUND QUESTIONS

1. Does this analogy in Scripture encourage you or confuse you? Do you see God's love in some of the hard changes you've endured or are enduring? Why?

2. When you encounter a hard change or unpleasant circumstances, are you more prone to believe that God is punishing you or loving you well? Why?

PRAYER NUDGE

Confess places in your life where you've felt like God was unjustly punishing you. Ask Him to show you whether or not your assessment was legitimate and open your heart to the possibility that even the hardest change you've walked through was a loving allowance from God. Ask God that His Holy Spirit alive in you might lead you to a better understanding of His love for you in the midst of these circumstances.

DAY 15
IT WILL ALL WORK TOGETHER FOR GOOD

I love the way Job's story ends – don't you? (Feel free to go back to Day 11 for a little refresher – or dig into Job 42:10-17)

God doesn't leave Job hanging. He doesn't punish him for his wrestling or questioning. He doesn't smite him and say, "You should've been fine through this. You shouldn't have felt any real pain if I truly sustained you."

But what does He do?

First, God accepts Job's prayers. He actually acknowledges the fact that Job spoke rightly of God when his friends didn't. He then urges Job to pray for his friends – to pray specifically that God would not deal with them according to their foolishness. Then Job prays and we are told God (graciously) accepts his prayers.

God doesn't stop there – because why would He? The second thing He does is so beautiful, so gracious and so kind that it legitimately brings tears to the corners of my eyes.

Job 42:10-11 (ESV) says, "And the Lord restored the fortunes of Job, when he had prayed for his friends. And the Lord gave Job twice as much as he had before. Then came to him all his brothers and sisters and all who had known him before and ate bread with him in his house. And they showed him sympathy and comforted him for all the evil that the Lord had brought upon him. And each of them gave him a piece of money and a ring of gold."

Can you picture this redemption? Can you see this scene in your head?

I am picturing a lonely guy leading up to this moment. A guy who had three less-than-awesome friends come comfort him in the wake of the most unthinkable tragedy and who, eventually, was left with God alone on his side. I picture him missing his kids, mourning the loss of the lives they once shared and throwing his hands up in the air above his grief-shaved head. I picture him going into the ring with God and going round for round with honest questions and tear-filled confessions.

And then I see this. A double blessing.

In a near-perfect picture of redemption, God shows up and reminds Job that He loves him and He is still in control.

We are uniquely positioned to see that God was in control the entire time. Remember, God allowed Satan to target Job and He set the ground rules (Job 1:12, 2:6). Satan was on God's playing field and there wasn't a single second where he had the upper hand.

The same is true in our lives in.

When I try to picture myself in Job's shoes, I fail. I can't picture that kind of tragedy, that kind of loss or that kind of grief. I cannot picture feeling so helpless, hopeless and out of control all at once. I cannot even begin to imagine what it would be like to walk the grief-stricken road he walked thousands of years ago.

To some degree, though, I can relate to feeling like my life was completely out of control. And I'm sure you can too.

I felt that way when I graduated college, when I went through that earth shattering breakup, when I was crippled by an anxiety and panic disorder during the first year of our marriage and when I changed jobs a year into our marriage.

In each of these scenarios, I had no idea how things would shake out or how God would show up and make things right. I knew the truth of Romans 8:28, that "for those who love God all things work together for good," but I couldn't see how it would happen.

Like Job, I wondered if there would be a "good" ending.

And maybe you've been there too.

Maybe you've wondered how God would restore an immensely broken area of your life or your store.

Maybe you've struggled to see how God would bring peace back to your family, your heart or your mind.

Maybe you've been so wronged by someone and you cannot make sense of how God could use the aftermath for good.

I don't share this story of Job to falsely promise you that God will double any sort of material possession you may've lost. I don't share this story to pump out more Christian pleasantries that say, "Life with Jesus is easy!" I don't know how God will redeem whatever messy change you've experienced in the past, are walking through now or will face in the future. I wish I could tell you – but I can't.

What I can tell you – and why I do share this story – is this:

God's character has not and will not change.

The same God who restored Job's losses and sweetly redeemed his pain is at work in your life.

The same God who allowed Job to die "an old man, full of days" is in control of your life.

The same God who promised us that all things work out for the good of those who love Him is speaking truth into your heart.

God's heart is to redeem. God's plans for us are good. Even when it hurts, even when it seems impossible – He is working all things together for our good and for His glory.

Will you trust that today?

And we know that for those who love God all things work together for good, for those who are called according to his purpose.

Romans 8:28 (ESV)

KICK AROUND QUESTIONS

1. Does Romans 8:28 seem true in your life – or does it sound like just another thing that Christians say to make themselves feel better when times are tough?

2. Jot down one situation or change in your life where you can look back and see Romans 8:28 ring true.

PRAYER NUDGE

Praise God for the promise of Romans 8:28 and thank Him for being a God who always makes good on His word. Talk to Him about one situation or change in your life that you are either encountering right now or are anticipating encountering in the near future. Tell Him your fears about it not working out for good and ask Him to increase your faith as you lean into the truth of Romans 8:28.

When You Choose Change

DAY 16
REMEMBER PAUL

Another story in the Bible where we see change play a key factor is in the life and ministry of Paul. Paul is credited with writing a good chunk of the New Testament and went on multiple missionary journeys to share the pure Gospel of Jesus Christ with the early church.

What you might not know about Paul is his history.

I invite you to read the book of Acts – it's a long book, but it's one that will help you understand the life and ministry of Paul. For today, here's a quick overview of some of the key points of Paul's life that we'll focus on for the next few days:

— Paul's (called Saul in certain parts of the Bible) first appearance in in the very same scene where we see the first Christian being killed for *being* a Christian (Acts 7:58). We are later told, by Paul himself, that he gave his approval by guarding the clothes of the people actually committing the murder (Acts 22:20).

— Paul (then, Saul) was out to get Christians. For much of his early life, he was not a believer and persecuted and injured Christians. It wasn't until a life-altering encounter with Jesus on his way to go wrangle up some more Christians to persecute that his life was changed. Go ahead and read Acts 9:1-19 in The Message version. It will paint a clear picture of what went on before and during his "conversion" to Christianity.

— After his encounter with Jesus, conversion and baptism, Saul eventually goes by Paul for the remainder of Scripture. It is under this name (Paul) that he writes a bulk of the New Testament, preaches and suffers for Christ's sake.

That's a fairly watered-down version of Saul's story – but the point we are really honing in on here is that Paul chose change. Yes – Jesus pursued Paul and chased down his heart with a ferocious grace. He was chosen by Jesus, won over by the Holy Spirit and by the unrelenting love of Christ.

But on some level, Paul complied.

On some level, Paul chose to forsake his old life of Christian-slaying darkness and to walk forward into the light where Jesus stood, calling.

Paul chose change. For the same reason we sometimes choose change – obedience. And just because he chose obedience, his whole life didn't fall into place.

So often we think that if we pursue God, if we are in His will and after His heart, the change we choose will be easy.

We think that if we end that relationship, it won't hurt.

We think if we enroll in this graduate program, our minutes will somehow effortlessly stretch to help us accomplish all we need.

We think if we sell all of our possessions and step into a life of full-time missions, we won't wrestle with feelings of inadequacy or loneliness.

We think if we finally decide to start saving sex for marriage, our sex life after walking down the aisle will automatically be steamy and romantic.

I wonder if Paul thought the same. I wonder if, at the point of his blindness, Paul thought choosing to lean into this change and follow Jesus would be easier than his old life. I wonder if – amidst his fervent praying – he thought walking into the light would be a cake walk.

I wonder if Paul fooled himself in the way we sometimes do.

I vividly remember when we got married, despite knowing in my heart of hearts that marriage WOULDN'T solve all my problems, thinking that in some ways, I'd just be happier. I remember thinking that the wedding stress would be gone so maybe-just-maybe there would be a weight removed from my chest that would free me from anxiety and panic.

When this didn't happen, I felt guilty.

In the same way, when I left my job in Corporate Marketing for a job in full-time ministry, I expected this change to lead me to a place of total vocational contentment in God. Yet in the beginning, I still felt challenged by the need for more: to be used more, to find more satisfaction in my 9-to-5 and to produce more.

We have this tendency to think that when we choose change by making a decision "for the better," life will just magically slip into place. We expect the change to show immediate results – whether it's feeling better, looking better, sleeping better, etc. – we almost always expect instant outcomes.

But like we will see with Paul, sometimes choosing change shakes out a little differently than we expected. Sometimes, just like when change chooses us, choosing change is yet another tool God uses to bring us deeper and closer and nearer to His heart.

The heart of man plans his way, but the Lord establishes his steps.

Proverbs 16:9 (ESV)

KICK AROUND QUESTIONS

1. Identify a time in your life when you chose a specific change, but it didn't pan out the way you planned.

2. What about this situation (or its outcome) surprised you? Were you disappointed? Shocked? Indifferent? Relieved? Why?

PRAYER NUDGE

Steal this prayer: Lord, I acknowledge that sometimes, I try to take the reins. When I make my own plans for my life – sometimes I am disappointed when things don't turn out the way I expected them to. I confess that sometimes I expect things to turn around when I make decisions out of obedience. When I fall into this thought pattern, God, remind me that You are not just in control – but that Your timing is perfect. Help me to remember that just because things don't go my way does not mean I am not pursuing Your perfect will for my life. In Jesus' Name, Amen.

DAY 17
IT TAKES TIME TO ADJUST

W e covered this a little bit, but when I first moved to Charlotte back in May 2013, I struggled to adjust to the newness of a city while at the same time I was struggling to let go of the familiarity of a dying love.

On one particular weekend in the first few months I was in Charlotte, I sat quiet in my little apartment and reflected on some of the changes that took place and were still taking place.

I thought about how no more than six months ago, the apartment I sat in was colored differently. Walls splattered with the paint and personality of another. Different appliances, different furniture and a different DVD collection. I thought about how, at some point, when he or she decided it was time to pack up and move on, it was scrubbed and vacuumed and tidied up just for me. I thought about how the painters came in – with buckets and tarps and rollers and brushes – and primed the walls into a fresh canvas that would give me an even fresher start. I thought about how my dad and I went up and down the steps about a half-million times, in the middle of the late-spring Carolina heat as we unpacked my two-door Honda Civic and unloaded 24 years of stuff into 767 square feet. I thought about how, for two days, my dad and my how-on-earth-did-I-get-roped-into-this friend, Scott, labored over modular furniture while I tried to learn the names of all the tools in my new toolbox. I thought about how each time they asked for the Phillip's head; I laughed and then seriously asked, "One more time… is that the one with the plus-sign on the end or the other one?" I thought about the looks they gave me and how they rolled their eyes and eventually just started asking me to bring them water and turn on the air conditioner.

I thought about how it felt driving my dad to the airport the morning of his flight back to New York, knowing that night would be the first time I'd sleep alone in my very own apartment. I thought about how I'd remember that night forever and probably tell my kids about it one day and lie through my teeth about how brave I was – just so they wouldn't be scared. I thought about how I cried on my way to work that first day alone and how I swore I'd never be comfortable in this new place so far away from the familiarity of thick smog and salty air. I thought about how there were moments when I clawed and scraped and scratched around for faces I might recognize – just people who knew me and who I could do life with, but things were complicated and I just couldn't call. I thought about how I felt homesick on Sundays when people had family dinners with their real-life moms and real-life dads while I sat around eating re-heated quinoa with the cast of my favorite TV show.

When I moved here, I wanted nothing more than a community of friends to call my people. I wanted nothing more than to have a life filled with cookouts and movie nights and dinner parties – but that didn't happen right away.

It took time. It took consistent effort. And it took believing that God was at work.

We see this happen to Paul, too. When he was gung-ho and ready to go preach Jesus to the world, everyone else was still a little bit skeptical of the sincerity of his conversion.

Take a peek at Acts 9:10-14 (ESV) below for a glimpse at some of the skepticism:

[10]Now there was a disciple at Damascus named Ananias. The Lord said to him in a vision, "Ananias." And he said, "Here I am, Lord." [11]And the Lord said to him, "Rise and go to the street called Straight, and at the house of Judas look for a man of Tarsus named Saul, for behold, he is praying, [12]and he has seen in a vision a man named Ananias come in and lay his hands on him so that he might regain his sight." [13]But Ananias answered, "Lord, I have heard from many about this man, how much evil he has done to your saints at Jerusalem. [14]And here he has authority from the chief priests to bind all who call on your name."

Ananias had Jesus Himself verifying Paul's conversion and yet, still, he doubted if it was sincere. Still, he was leery of any association with this man. Eventually he goes and lays hands on Paul – but I can't help but wonder if he was still hesitant.

In all this we see this truth: The vision Paul had for his new life took a little bit of time to shake out. We're told Paul spends a few days with disciples in Damascus, before going to preach the Gospel. He wasn't instantly accepted. His past was not instantly forgotten by his new peers. It took some time for Paul to gain the trust of those around him and to gain momentum as he preached.

The same is true for us, right? Even when we are excited about the change we are choosing – it still takes time to "feel" normal again. Sometimes we have these "pinch yourself" moments where we cannot believe this is the life we are living (in a positive way) and other times we start to panic when things don't pan out according to plan right away.

Either way – we must remember that God is never early and never late. He is always right on time – and as we adjust to the change we choose, He is faithful to settle us in change in His perfect timing.

For everything there is a season, and a time for every matter under heaven.

Ecclesiastes 3:1 (ESV)

KICK AROUND QUESTIONS

1. What was a change you chose that resulted in a hard or uncomfortable adjustment period? Write about what made it difficult. (Some examples include: going to college, moving to a new city, ending or starting a relationship, taking a new job, etc.)

2. In the past, when you've chosen something that was followed by a natural adjustment period, did you rush the adjustment along – or did you lean into God in the midst of the discomfort? There's no wrong answer! Just be honest!

PRAYER NUDGE

Ask God to show you ways you can make the most out of some of life's natural adjustment periods. Get quiet before Him and listen as He prompts you to look for ways you can draw near to Him when things get hard – but also as He leads you outside of your comfort zone during these seasons.

DAY 18
RESISTANCE IS EXPECTED

Yesterday we started talking about some of the ways Paul faced resistance in his chosen change, but what we covered was just the tip of the iceberg.

Even though Paul spent "a few days" with the disciples in Damascus, they still weren't sure they could trust him. They said things like, "Isn't this the man who wreaked havoc in Jerusalem among the believers? And didn't he come here to do the same thing—arrest us and drag us off to jail in Jerusalem for sentencing by the high priests?" (Acts 9:21, MSG)

Again – this is after Jesus Himself vouched for Paul's sincerity in conversion to Ananias – yet they still struggled to believe him.

But Paul didn't let their lack of support stop him. He went head-on into his calling and began preaching the Gospel – wanting nothing more than for the Jews in Damascus to know that Jesus was the Messiah they'd been waiting for.

Paul's disregard for opposition to his chosen change is a prime example of God-given courage – and it's something we should be envious for in our own lives.

When I left my corporate job in 2017, for the most part my decision was deeply understood and graciously celebrated. I was met with support from even the most unlikely of places and was so excited to feel like others were onboard with me taking the plunge into full-time ministry.

But there were plenty of people who didn't get it. And there were even people who felt the need to communicate their displeasure.

"You're throwing away your career, Diana," someone said.

They followed it up with, "I think this is a mistake. I think you will regret this one day."

Ouch.

Even though I was set in my decision – even though I'd prayed fervently about the change I was choosing and felt affirmed in the choice I was making – the disapproval still rattled me.

I love how Paul just doesn't care.

I love how Paul got a word from God and just went for it. I love how there wasn't anything or anyone who could keep him from walking the divine path God set before him.

I love how their disapproval didn't faze him one bit and, instead, went straight to preaching right there in Damascus.

I can't help but be both inspired and convicted by this sort of assurance we see in Paul. I can't help but wonder how I would've reacted if I was in Paul's shoes.

Would I be so consumed with gaining the approval of the others on my team that I would've missed out on the immediate opportunities in front of me? Or would I trust the plan Jesus revealed to me in the days prior and just pursue it immediately and relentlessly?

I'm not sure if this is a symptom of being harder on ourselves than we are on anyone else – but I sometimes forget that I'm not the only one who sometimes struggles to deal with change. Sometimes, I forget that the people around me – the ones who are affected by my chosen change – also may struggle with it. And I think that is what prompts people to speak up when we make choices that will put them in change's path too.

Maybe you decided not to go to college or not to major in the area your parents wanted you to.

Maybe you broke up with the guy who all of your friends loved you with.

Maybe you took your name out of the hat for a promotion your coworkers think you'd be great for.

Maybe you left the job with a promising salary and retirement plan.

Change doesn't just rattle us – but it rattles the people closest to us. It doesn't just disrupt our ecosystem, but it shakes up the ecosystems around us, too. And sometimes, the people around us react to the changes we choose in ways that don't exactly feel the most supportive.

If you've ever found yourself in that place, hear this:

We live to please God, not man. It's hard and it's uncomfortable and sometimes, it really, really stinks – but when we remember that our obedience to God and His promptings means more than any human's approval or blessing – we are storing up treasures in Heaven that we cannot even begin to imagine.

The one who hears you hears me, and the one who rejects you rejects me, and the one who rejects me rejects him who sent me.

Luke 10:16 (ESV)

ROUND QUESTIONS

1. Was there ever a time in your life when you made an unpopular decision? Who disapproved of your decision and why?

2. When you feel God leading you to make a decision, do you react like Paul naturally? Or do you find yourself tempted to try and adjust the prompting to please those closest to you?

PRAYER NUDGE

Get humble before God and ask Him to help you desire to please Him more than any other person in your life. Ask Him to show you how to love and honor those around you without being dependent on their approval. Pray for a boldness that matches your desire to be obedient and thank God in advance for answering.

DAY 19
IT'S NOT ALWAYS WHAT YOU EXPECT

P eople will tell you that marriage doesn't fix you – and when you hear it, you will think, "I know. I get it." At least that's how I reacted.

When I was single, when I was dating someone, when Tyler and I were engaged – it was that piece of advice married people would constantly pass out as if to say, "Pump the breaks. Deal with the junk. It won't go away on its own." And you know what? I believed them.

Logistically, I knew marriage wouldn't solve my problems, heal past hurts or abolish my insecurities. But my completely hidden and unexpressed response to their wisdom?

"Yeah, but you're married. You don't get it. How could you have any problems being married anyway?"

Well – I can now say that I ate some serious crow.

Because those old married people who gave unsolicited advice about marriage and problems and junk and joy? They were right.

Marriage doesn't solve your problems. I repeat, marriage doesn't solve your problems.

Selfish? Marriage will magnify that.

Insecure? Marriage will expose that mess too.

Bad habits? Old vices? Deep-seeded pressure points? Check, check, check.

I knew marriage wouldn't solve problems – but I took it one step further: I thought those problems would just go away.

And spoiler alert: They didn't. Spoiler alert: They're heightened. Spoiler alert: I'm flawed and selfish and insecure and have pressure points and wounds just like the rest of us.

Deep down – my expectation of marriage wasn't that it would solve my problems, but that by getting something I had so deeply desired for so long, my problems would just disappear.

And that expectation? It wasn't met.

I wonder how Paul felt when he was met with immediate resistance. We're told in Scripture that Jesus will show Paul how much he must suffer for His (Jesus') name's sake (Acts 9:16), but to my knowledge, we're never actually told what or how Jesus revealed this truth.

Did He reveal this truth by allowing Paul to go through deep suffering (e.g., being whipped, being beaten, enduring multiple shipwrecks, being robbed, imprisonment, etc.) as he brought the Gospel to the ends of the earth? And even if Jesus had a one-on-one conversation not recorded in Scripture where He told Paul the extent of the suffering he would endure – do you think Paul could really grasp it before it happened?

Like the people who told me – from their own experience – that marriage would expose sin in me like no other relationship – would he try to believe, or even think he believed them, but then when push came to shove – would he be surprised?

When we step into change – when we choose something for our lives that we are excited about, looking forward to or anticipating greatly – sometimes, we operate under the illusion that getting this aspect of our life "right" will prompt all other areas of our lives to follow suit and fall into place. Sometimes, we put the season or place this change will bring us to on a pedestal and make an idol out of what we hope will come from it.

And sometimes, when things don't manifest exactly how we expected them to – the disappointment derails us. In the rubble of unmet expectations, we crumble beneath the reality that life didn't magically become utopian.

When we look at Paul, though, and when we look at the big narrative surrounding his life and ministry, we can pick out pieces of his story where his unmet expectations did nothing but propel him forward into purpose.

Not only does he warn Timothy, his mentee and ministry partner, of the certainty of prosecution (2 Timothy 3:12), but he urges him to continue in pursuit of preaching the Gospel to as many who will listen – for a time was coming when hearts would no longer be open to the message (2 Timothy 4:3-5). Paul refocuses both himself and Timothy on the reason they were enduring these sufferings in the first place as a means to spur them on in their ministry.

You see, when we are grappling with unmet expectations of a chosen change, we can't be so quick to forget why we stepped into this change in the first place.

I married Tyler because I love him more than any string of words and punctuation could ever say. I have been forever changed by his selfless love, tender care and unending patience. I have seen the depths of his heart for people, for me

– and more importantly, for Jesus. When I found myself in a dark place at the beginning of our marriage – I had to remember all of these things. I had to remember who I married and why I married him. And when I did – I was able to share the deepest parts of me with my new husband and walk through the rubble with him by my side.

Not that I am speaking of being in need, for I have learned in whatever situation I am to be content. I know how to be brought low, and I know how to abound. In any and every circumstance, I have learned the secret of facing plenty and hunger, abundance and need.

Philippians 4:11-12 (ESV)

KICK AROUND QUESTIONS

1. Have you ever wondered why you made a change? Have you ever been so exhausted by the consequences (good or bad) of a chosen change that you've doubted if you ever should've made the decision in the first place?

2. Do you feel like you typically have healthy expectations when you make decisions or changes? Or do you feel like you typically over or under shoot things by imagining them far worse or far better than expected?

PRAYER NUDGE

Talk to God about ways your expectations can be centered around Him. Ask Him, like Paul states in Philippians 4, to show you how to be content in all circumstances. Tap into the idea of a holy contentment and journal out some of the ways God satisfies you in any and every circumstance.

DAY 20
IT WILL ALL WORK TOGETHER FOR GOOD

When we look at Paul's life, ministry, sufferings and trials – it's safe to say we can see the good that came from it, right? Despite the opposition and the unmet expectations, we can see how God used every last bit of Paul's journey for His glory, amen?
Just to name a few…

— Even Paul's (Saul's) pre-conversion days were used for good! After Stephen's death (which Saul condoned, remember?), Christians in Jerusalem were scattered to surrounding regions in efforts to squash Christianity. What did they do in those surrounding regions, though? They preached the Gospel there! (Acts 8:4)

— Despite persecution, Paul went before Gentiles (non-Jewish people) and even kings to preach the Gospel. (Acts 9:15, Romans 15:20-21)

— Paul's writings make up nearly half of the New Testament and live on for the benefit and encouragement of Christians all over the world. (2 Timothy 3:16, 2 Peter 1:20-21)

We can easily look at Paul's story and see God's fingerprint over every detail. Despite the shipwrecks, despite the imprisonment, despite the opposition – we can see how God's purpose ultimately prevailed and how Paul truly was used as the chosen instrument Jesus said he would be.

But when we look at our lives, can we see the same? And if we can see the same – can we see it as easily?

When we choose obedience and accept a job with a 35% pay cut – do we see God's hand six-months in when our savings account is dwindling?

When we choose obedience and move to a new city where we only know a handful of people – do we see God's hand when we encounter feelings of regret?

When we choose obedience and end a relationship – do we see God's hand when the freedom we anticipated feeling luxurious instead feels a lot like loneliness?

If you're anything like me, you find it so stinkin' easy to extract the good from other peoples' stories, from other peoples' chosen changes and yet, you find it so stinkin' hard to do the same for your own life.

At different points in my life, I've had conversation after conversation with people about the season of change or the transition they were walking through. Almost instantaneously, I've been able to identify the way God might be doling out His grace in the midst of the situation. It's like the "good" of their chosen change jumped up and smacked me in the face.

Graduating college and leaving all of your friends behind while also not knowing what the heck you're doing with your life? Oh girl! God is inviting you to trust Him in this. It's in these seasons where we develop such a sweet intimacy with Him!

Getting married and not sure you can tell your husband THAT part of your story? Being fully known and fully loved is one of the biggest blessings of marriage! Lean into this call to vulnerability, friend. I promise you it will be worth it.

Took a new job and unsure of how you'll make ends meet financially? This is your opportunity to trust in God's provision, girl. How would He show up if we didn't need Him? Needing Him for practical things like financial provision is such a perfect set up for Him to show up BIG!

See? I can do this all day – the whole let-me-call-out-the-blessings-in-your-situation-while-my-eyes-go-blurry-looking-for-my-own thing.

And I don't think I'm alone in this.

When we choose change – I think there are two things we need to remember.

The first is this: We can't mess up the plan. We simply can't thwart God's plan for our lives because He is sovereign. (Sovereign is just a fancy way of saying He is in control.) We don't need to obsess over the details of the why's and the how's and the when's in stepping into change because God's got all of that taken care of and we have the freedom to live wildly into that grace.

The second thing I would tell you is this: We only see a fraction of the plan. We only see flickers of His glory in our lives, on this side of eternity, and in between those flickers we get distracted by life.

I once heard a pastor use an illustration of these sorts of distractions by placing a water bottle in front of his face.

"This," he said holding the water bottle as close to his nose as possible. "This is your problem. This is whatever you're walking through. It's right in front of you and it's all you can see. You obsess over it. It's all you think about. When you wake up in the morning, it's the first thing you see and before you go to bed at night, it's the last thing you see."

He then took the water bottle and moved it as far away from his face as his arm would let him.

"But this – this is perspective. When we take a step back from whatever it is in front of us – whether it's by intentional reflection or by being removed from it by time – we can see the whole picture. We can see what's really going on – not just focus on this problem right in front of us."

When we walk through chosen change – we need to do all we can to back up that water bottle. We need to do all we can to gain a little perspective, focus on the big picture and realize that His plan is bigger and better and more trustworthy than anything we could ever think up.

He is faithful – only, ever, always faithful – to keep His promises. And He promises it will all work out for our good.

And we know that for those who love God all things work together for good, for those who are called according to his purpose.

Romans 8:28 (ESV)

KICK AROUND QUESTIONS

1. You'll notice today's verse is a repeat from Day 15. It's that important that I want you to hear it twice. In the past five days, has your feeling toward this verse or it's truth changed?

2. In what ways do you struggle to believe this to be true in instances where you are responsible for a chosen change? Do you believe God can work even some of our less-than-good decisions for our good?

PRAYER NUDGE

Praise God for the promise of Romans 8:28 and thank Him again for being a God who always makes good on His word. Revisit your prayer from Day 15 and record some of the ways God has worked in your heart and life since then.

When You Long For Change

DAY 21
LOOK FOR BEAUTY IN THE MUNDANE

I f you were to come and shadow me for a week – here's a little bit of what our schedule would look like:

— On the good Monday mornings, we'd get up and spend some sweet time with coffee and Jesus before making a smoothie and heading out the door. You'd sit in a couple meetings with me, catch up on a flurry of emails and come home to make dinner for a group of 13 of the best girls Charlotte's got to offer. You'd sit in my living room with said girls and help me lead a discussion about Jesus and how His love for us is relevant even in 2018. After they leave, you'd help Tyler and I tidy up the kitchen and listen to us fill each other in on the details of our days. We'd pour a glass of wine and sit on the couch for 15-minutes or so before heading up to bed.

— Tuesday looks a lot like Monday – except this time instead of dinner for 13, it's dinner for two – and Tyler and I would have a night to ourselves at home. We'd probably take our pup, Elliot, for a walk to the dog park and then come home for a relaxing night of Netflix.

— Wednesday? Coffee, Jesus, smoothie, work, dinner, home. Most Wednesday nights we hang out with the college kids from our church, but we're typically home by 9 and in bed by 10:30.

— Thursday and Fridays look pretty much the same – except Fridays I work from home and usually get a workout class in during my lunch hour.

— Our weekends are filled with home projects, laundry and trips to grocery stores. More walks for the pup, more times with friends, church and reading.

At first glance – doesn't this seem kind of… monotonous? I love – absolutely love – the life God has blessed me with. Honestly, I would not trade a single thing for an ounce more or an ounce less of anything. But I do go through phrases thinking, "Hmmm. There sure is a lot of mundane in this life, isn't there?"

I mean, if I had a dollar for every time I loaded or unloaded the dishwasher, folded up the giant throw blanket that is often sprawled across our couch, swapped out dirty damp towels for clean ones, or wiped down our countertops after making dinner – I'd be rolling in singles, ladies.

There is just so much – SO MUCH – in life that feels like we have the "Repeat" button on. There are so many things in this life that have become routine, survival-type tasks that, if I'm not careful, I stop appreciating. And when I stop appreciating what's around me? I keep looking ahead to the next thing – to some sort of change to bring about excitement – and I stop living in the very place God's placed me.

Confession time: I've done this most recently in my insatiable desire to start a family with Tyler. If you know me or have even had just one conversation with me, you know that more than anything – I long to be a mom. Tyler and I have had innumerable conversations about expanding our family and we are trusting God's timing for our dreams to come to fruition – but if I'm honest, it's super hard for me to wait. (Can anyone relate?)

The wait has been so hard for me, that in the monotonous places of our everyday life in this stage – I've caught myself daydreaming about what it would look like if we had a newborn in our home.

Laying on the couch at night watching Netflix? *Oh, wouldn't that be so much sweeter with a little baby burrito on my chest?* Fixing dinner before Tyler gets home? *Imagine what this would be like while wearing a baby, Diana!* Taking Elliot for a Saturday walk after lunch? *How sweet would this be if we were pushing one of those fancy jogging strollers?*

I know. It sounds crazy. I'm sure I sound a certain type of delusional as you read these words – but they're honest and they're vulnerable and I think they illustrate how much we can miss when we long for change that hasn't yet found us.

Sometimes, the change we so earnestly long for can cause us to inadvertently stop cherishing the very gifts God has given us in the here and now.

Like my sweet Tyler. It pains me to think that in my intense desire to be a mom, he's ever felt like being his wife wasn't enough for me. It makes my heart hurt when I think of how unappreciated I've made him feel when all I can do is talk about being a mom.

Here's the truth, friend: Mundane isn't bad. It gets a bad rap these days when all we ever see is people hashtagging their grand adventures – but I believe with all my heart that God grows us in the mundane if we let Him. The mundane? It's beautiful. Not in a cliché way and not in a wishful-thinking way either.

The mundane is beautiful because it's filled with small moments of God's big graces. The mundane is beautiful because it's filled with constant reminders of God's grand provision and His promise to sustain us. The mundane is beautiful because it's a soft place to land, it's steady, it's constant – and it points us straight to Him.

And whatever you do, in word or deed, do everything in the name of the Lord Jesus, giving thanks to God the Father through him.

Colossians 3:17 (ESV)

KICK AROUND QUESTIONS

1. Are there parts of your life that feel mundane, routine or downright boring? Jot 'em down below.

2. In these tasks or habits of your life, what are some ways you can look for God's grace and beauty as you carry them out?

PRAYER NUDGE

Thank God for the life you have – for every aspect of it, good or bad. Ask Him to show you how to delight in the small and mundane moments and for a greater appreciation of the grace He's poured out to you. As you look ahead to what's next in your life – as you desire whatever is up ahead – ask Him to enable you to experience deep contentment in the present.

DAY 22
TRUST GOD'S TIMING

I'm going to air out some more dirty laundry today. I figured since we're already 22 days into this journey – I can trust you with some of the messy parts of my heart, right?

I sometimes get really, really frustrated by some of the things we say to each other as Christians. Even more than that, I sometimes get really frustrated by the things we (Christians) say to others who maybe don't walk with Jesus. Sometimes, I think even the most well-meaning phrases can be the source of hurt in our stories.

Just in case you need some examples – the title of this chapter should point you in the right direction. Trust God's timing.

I will be the first to say that I have uttered this statement. In moments where I have not known what to say, in moments when I felt like I had to say something yet just couldn't find any words to come to my lips – I have whispered these three words. And almost immediately, I've wondered if being uncomfortable with silence and just filling the space with words did more harm than good.

The thing about Biblical truths and Christian quips is that a lot of the time they don't tell the whole story. Sometimes, they brush over the meat of the why… like, in this case why we should be a people, a generation, who trusts God's perfect timing.

It's not, "Trust God's timing because it will happen, you just need to wait a little bit longer."

It's not, "Trust God's timing because soon enough you will find exactly what you're hoping for."

It's not, "Trust God's timing because you just need to clean your act up a little bit before He blesses you."

None of those inferred meanings are based in Biblical truth.

When we say, "Trust God's timing," I feel like we should almost always follow up with the truth about His heart.

Why? Because when you're in the wait, God's timing doesn't always super obviously align with His character – and when someone tells you, "Trust God's timing" when you're two years into trying to conceive a baby or single at 38, you may wonder, "Why?"

I feel like we need to know the "why" behind these sorts of statements. Not just so we can be prepared to answer when people ask – but because that extra layer of truth ministers to our own hearts when we find ourselves asking the same question.

Trust God's timing. Why? Because He is good (Psalm 25:8) even when we don't feel like He is.

Trust God's timing. Why? Because He is the Creator of all things (Colossians 1:16) and He is in control.

Trust God's timing. Why? Because He Himself is the very definition and essence of love (1 John 4:8) and He loves you.

Trust God's timing. Why? Because He is trustworthy (Psalm 22:4-5) and we see it over and over again in Scripture.

When we understand God's character, we are better positioned to trust His timing.

Those who trust in the LORD are like Mount Zion, which cannot be moved, but abides forever.

Psalm 125:1 (ESV)

KICK AROUND QUESTIONS

1. What is one thing you need to surrender to God and say, "I trust your timing," about?

2. Write down three things that make it hard for you to trust God's timing. (Be honest – there's no shame, girl!)

PRAYER NUDGE

Ask God to give you brave face and a glad heart as you lay down your answer to question 1 at His feet. Ask Him to show you that He knows – more than anyone – what true surrender looks like, because He surrendered His Son to the cross. Thank Him for leading the way in surrender.

DAY 23
REMEMBER HIS FAITHFULNESS

One of my favorite pieces of imagery in the Bible is found in the Old Testament book of Joshua. It spans from Joshua 3 and Joshua 4 – but it's roots can be traced all the way back through Genesis.

To give you a super quick little recap of what's going on and why it's so significant, here's a quick rundown:

God chose Abraham and told him that he would be the father of many nations and dwell in the land He chose for them. Abraham's family becomes the nation of Israel, but the Israelites end up enslaved in Egypt – not in the Promised Land God spoke of with Abraham. Eventually, the Israelites are rescued (out of Egypt and slavery) by Moses. Moses leads the Israelites out of Israel and through the wilderness, where they receive the Ten Commandments. Moses dies just before the Israelites cross the Jordan River into the Promised Land. Joshua takes over as the new leader of Israel and leads the Israelites across the Jordan River. Just like the Red Sea parted for Moses, the Jordan River parts for the Israelites and they enter into the Promised Land.

To better capture the part of the narrative we're focusing on today, I've included The Message translation of Joshua 4:1-9 below:

> When the whole nation was finally across, God spoke to Joshua: "Select twelve men from the people, a man from each tribe, and tell them, 'From right here, the middle of the Jordan where the feet of the priests are standing firm, take twelve stones. Carry them across with you and set them down in the place where you camp tonight.'"

> Joshua called out the twelve men whom he selected from the People of Israel, one man from each tribe. Joshua directed them, "Cross to the middle of the Jordan and take your place in front of the Chest of God, your God. Each of you heft a stone to your shoulder, a stone for each of the tribes of the People of Israel, so you'll have something later to mark the occasion. When your children ask you, 'What are these stones to you?' you'll say, 'The flow of the Jordan was stopped in front of the Chest of the Covenant of God as it crossed the Jordan—stopped in its tracks. These stones are a permanent memorial for the People of Israel.'"

> The People of Israel did exactly as Joshua commanded: They took twelve stones from the middle of the Jordan—a stone for each of the twelve tribes, just as God had instructed Joshua—carried them across with them to the camp and set them down there. Joshua set up the twelve stones taken from the middle of the Jordan that had marked the place where the priests who carried the Chest of the Covenant had stood. They are still there today. (Joshua 4:1-9 [MSG])

Joshua knows he is dealing with a forgetful people. He knows he is leading the same nation who complained when they were brought out of slavery in Egypt (Exodus 14:10-14), the same people who complained about God's provision in the wilderness (Numbers 11:1-9). Despite God's constant provision, the Israelites constantly grumbled.

Joshua doesn't want the Israelites to forget this – God's fulfilment of His age-old promise with Abraham. He fulfilled His covenant. And Joshua knew that Israel was prone to forgetting the provision when times got tough.

I can't look at the Israelites and not see my own heart in their tendencies. I can't read these stories of their incessant complaints and not think, "Woof. This is me."

Like Israel, I am kept alive by a heart that beats with forgetfulness. When I long for change and when I yearn for what's ahead, I become so obsessed with a future season that I tend to forget God's faithfulness in past seasons.

Joshua's solution? Make a monument. Drag out physical stones marking God's faithfulness so that when future generations say, "Hey. What are those piles of stones for?" they would remember.

I've tried to take a page out of Joshua's book here and cultivate my own stone monuments of God's faithfulness. For me, this looks like intentional journaling – in all seasons. By journaling in hard seasons, I see the things I fervently prayed for. By journaling in joyful seasons, I see the way the Lord's answered previous prayers (for better or for worse) and catch glimpses of His faithfulness.

Today, be on the lookout for ways you can gather some stones. Look for ways God has shown up and is showing up in your story. Don't forget His faithfulness.

I will remember the deeds of the LORD; yes, I will remember your wonders of old.

Psalm 77:11 (ESV)

KICK AROUND QUESTIONS

1. Take five to ten minutes to list out some "stones" in your own life. Record God's faithfulness in your journal as a place to look back on in times of doubt.

2. What are some of the ways you can cultivate a spirit of remembrance daily?

PRAYER NUDGE

Take a look at the list you made for question 1 and thank God, specifically, for each "stone." Ask Him to gently convict you when you fall into a state of forgetfulness and to sweetly remind you of the ways He's shown up BIG in your own story.

DAY 24
LONG FOR GOD MORE

I'm sure by now you get the gist – but I have a tendency to become fixated on things.

My weight or appearance.
Getting married.
Being a mom.

You name it. If it's a good thing and I want it – I am prone to becoming obsessed with the desire. I'm just going to call it like it is here and rob the enemy of some power by exercising confession, okay?

I have the tendency to make things idols. I've heard it said that we make things idols when we make good things the ultimate things. I confess, here to you today, that I do that sometimes.

I have spent chunks of my life being so fixated on the next stage, the next milestone, the next desire being fulfilled, that I look back with a little bit of regret when I come to terms with some of the good things I wasn't fully present for.

For whatever reason, I struggle to find that healthy balance between working toward whatever it is I want and becoming 100% obsessed with obtaining it. I get so distracted by whatever is (or whatever I want to be) around the corner that it becomes all I can focus on and all I think or talk about. It is this very tendency that robs me of the fullness God has for me in the season I am in. But we've covered this, right?

More than robbing me of the fullness God has for me in the here in now, this "around the corner thinking" (as I've heard it aptly named), reveals something deeper than my inability to enjoy the present. It reveals the things, places, people or statuses in my life that I've made into idols.

Again, in the spirit of honesty and full disclosure, there've been seasons of my life where I've recognized a particular desire as an idol and I wasn't quite sure what to do about it once I realized I was idolizing something. When I was younger, I heard a lot of older Christians talk about "casting down idols" – and I think we even sang songs about it – but I never truly grasped what it meant. The Bible talks a good bit about idolatry (usually in the form of prohibiting the creation or worship of statues made in representation of other gods), but I never wrestled with idolatry in that way. The manifestation in my life, and in many of our lives, is much different in 2018. We don't build altars to foreign gods or carve spiritual statues out of gold.

That said, for a while, I grappled with how to lay down a contemporary idol – like the desire to be married or to be a mom – and to truly surrender it to the Lord.

How could I stop myself from desiring something?
How could I just stop wanting something to happen in my life?

If we zoom out a little bit and take it back to the working definition above (e.g., making good things ultimate things), the recipe for "casting down" idols is simple: Want God more.

My pastor talks about this concept a lot – specifically when he talks about addiction. I've heard him say a number of times that the only way to beat an addiction is to love something more than that to which you are addicted.

The same is true for us when we want something more than we want God; when we love the idea of something more than we love Him.

The only way to beat idolatry is to safeguard our hearts and minds against loving anything more than we love our God. A simple, yet profound and powerful, way that I've cultivated this deep love for God is to just get really honest before Him and ask Him for it.

In my desperation, I've prayed a prayer similar to the one below – and God, as He always does, showed up.

Dear Lord,

I confess to you that I am a sinner – a broken and messed up sinner – and because of this, I am so guilty of putting things before You. I am so guilty of wanting things more than You and of loving things more than You. I confess these to You and ask You for your forgiveness – and God, You are so faithful and so loving to forgive me. I thank You even now for Your unending grace.

God, I so humbly ask that You create in me a hunger that only You can satisfy.

I ask that You'd create in me an insatiable craving for Your word and for the desire to spend time with You.

I ask that where my eyes are so prone to looking left or right, You would tenderly nudge me to look straight ahead and lock eyes with You.

I ask that You would continue to call me to Yourself –
over and over again – and stir my affections and love for
You in a way that is unrivaled.

I love You, Lord. Help me to think, love and make
decisions like it is the truest thing about me.

In Jesus' name, Amen.

*But seek first the kingdom of God and his
righteousness, and all these things will be added to
you.*

Matthew 6:33 (ESV)

KICK AROUND QUESTIONS

1. Do you have any contemporary idols in your life?
    Take an honest assessment of your priorities – not
    just how you spend your time, but what you think
    about most. Is God at the top of your list?

2. What are some ways you can safeguard your heart
    against idolatry?

PRAYER NUDGE

Use the prayer above as a launching point for your
prayer today. Feel free to steal it completely, modify it or
write it out in your own words.

DAY 25
ASK FOR IT

I'm sure you've heard the idea of the "Name It, Claim It" or prosperity gospel – and it's the whole idea that financial prosperity and physical wellbeing are always the will of God for people on this side of eternity. Christians who subscribe to this belief often think that positive talk, faith and tithing to the church will heap God's material abundance on their lives. Especially if we ask for it.

> Wealth.
> Health.
> Happiness.

It's a pervasive belief system that we should work to guard ourselves from as, in my opinion, it does not align with Scripture; however, in contemporary Christianity, it seems as though we've made a bit of an overcorrection.

How so? We don't ask for anything.

Now – before we move on, hear this: What I'm about to say to you is being said by a pioneer, not a preacher. I am in the trenches with you on this – imperfect, wading through and asking God for grace upon grace along the way. Got it? Okay.

Prayer is the most underutilized resource we have access to. Plain and simple: We don't use it enough.

Again, speaking as someone who's right there with you in the category of "those who probably don't pray enough," I think we count God out before we even talk to God. Some excuses you may find yourself using… just to name a few:

— This is too small to bring to God. I shouldn't bother Him with something like this. There are other people who need Him more right now.
— This is way too big to bring to God. I know He can do anything, but there's just no way this will ever come to fruition. It's impossible.
— I'm sure God is sick of me talking about this.

Or my personal sin trap: I don't need to spend time praying about this – God knows my heart.

Because I believe God is omniscient (the fancy Christian way of saying that He knows everything), I can sometimes use that as a subconscious excuse to not pray. Not because I don't want to or because I don't desire intimacy with God – but because I simply don't feel the need to.

If God knows everything, if He "knows the desires of my heart," why do I need to present my desires to Him?

Why would I spend time asking for something if God already knows that I desire it so deeply?

You see, I think we've made a tragic assumption as Christians – as a culture – that prayer is about changing our circumstances instead of changing our hearts. I think we've equated praying with getting answers rather than being with the Answer.

If prayer is our primary way to communicate with God – then it's our primary way of being with God, too. And in this being with Him – our hearts often change.

Maybe we keep desiring whatever it is that brought us to our knees in the first place – and that's great! But many times, our perspective changes and we begin to view God as a friend who walks through the desire with us, instead of the genie who's contemplating granting it to us or not. Instead of our desire being the ultimate thing – we see it as an overflow of His goodness and know that whether or not we "get it," we are sustained and cared for by His grace.

Or maybe our desire changes.

Maybe instead of wanting to mend a relationship with someone you maybe shouldn't be dating, God reveals His heart for your future marriage.

Maybe instead of continuing to pray for a promotion, God blesses you with a spirit of contentment and reinvigorated purpose right where He has you.

Maybe instead of desiring a change of scenery, He shows you exactly why He wants you to stay put.

When we draw near to God in prayer, we shouldn't expect a transactional answer to a problem we're stuck in. God is not the barista behind the counter who hands us a latte when we hand him a five-dollar bill. Grace doesn't operate that way.

Drawing near to God is an experience, not a business deal.

We don't draw near so we get what we want – we draw near so He gets what He wants: our hearts and our holiness.

And even in seasons where we desire nothing more than some specific change – our prayer lives can be chock full of praises and declarations of His goodness because He is on the move.

We can approach God's throne with requests of all kinds – big, little, and everything in between – in fact, He wants us to. But when we do it – our posture must be rooted in the truth that no matter what we're asking for, just talking to God gives us so much more.

Rejoice always, pray without ceasing, give thanks in all circumstances; for this is the will of God in Christ Jesus for you.

1 Thessalonians 5:16-18 (ESV)

KICK AROUND QUESTIONS

1. What does your prayer life look like? Be honest –
    do you pray regularly? Daily? Weekly? When you
    need something? When everything's good?

2. What are some things that keep you from praying?

PRAYER NUDGE

Ask God to create an insatiable desire for intimacy with
Him in your soul. Ask Him to give you a hunger for
communion with Him and for your heart toward prayer to
become more committed than ever before. Ask God to
show you ways you can continually be talking to Him
throughout the day and journal about some ways you've
struggled to ask Him for certain things in the past.

Identify the Constants

DAY 26
GOD'S IDENTITY

In the middle of change, it's perhaps more important than ever to be rooted in the permanence of God's character and identity. When the waters are rising up around us and we are kicking our little legs as fast as we can to keep our head above the waves – our continued buoyancy is wholly dependent on who God is.

Without a firm grasp on who He is and how He acts toward us, overwhelm takes hold and before we know it, waves are crashing down on every side, our arms fly up over our head and we begin to spin and sink.

I'm not sure where you are in your faith – if you've been a follower of Jesus for years and years, if you're new to the whole Christianity thing, or if you're not sure about any of it at all – but I do know that the Bible can seem really intimidating sometimes. I know that no matter where you are in your journey, it can be hard to open the Bible and really soak up what it says about who God is.

So here's a little taste…

— He is the Creator of the Universe. (Genesis 1:1)
— He is holy. (Isaiah 43:15)
— He is without rival or equal. (Isaiah 40:25)
— He is loving. (1 John 4:8)
— He is just. (Deuteronomy 32:4)
— He is kind. (Psalm 117:2)
— He is faithful to keep His promises. (Hebrews 10:23)
— He is all powerful and in control. (Psalm 115:3)
— He is the one who parts waters. (Exodus 14:21)
— He is the one who speaks to the wind and calms the seas. (Matthew 8:23-27)
— He is the one who changes hearts. (Ezekiel 11:19)
— He is the one who heals lepers. (Luke 17:11-19)
— He is the one who sees the depth of our brokenness and stands by us still. (John 4)
— He is the one who calls the dead back to life. (John 11:43-44)
— He is unchanging. (James 1:17)

The list goes on and on and the truth is, we could never fully describe God with our human words or fully grasp Him with our human minds – but through His word, the Bible, we can know Him.

I believe that one of the main ways the enemy renders us impotent in our faith is by keeping us from God's word. He'll plant lies in our heads like we are not scholarly enough to understand it or not educated enough to dig in on our own.

He'll tempt us to believe that because we didn't grow up in Christian homes or Sunday School classes that we are disqualified from the ranks of those who understand the Bible.

He'll get extra creative and try to convince us that the Bible is just an old and irrelevant collection of made up stories with no value to our lives.

Hear this loud and clear, sister: None of that is true. Not even a little bit.

The Bible is FULL of stories and testimonies that back up all of the little one-liners about God's character above. There are hundreds of examples of His faithfulness in spite of our continual unfaithfulness. There are hundreds more examples of His holiness and His love and the way they act together as a catalyst for the saving work of Jesus. And though all of these examples occurred long ago – God hasn't changed, and He never will.

The realization that God is unchanging, is constant and permanent has been a great source of comfort to me amidst some of life's more challenging seasons of transition. We've already covered the part where we realize we're not in control – and even though I know that to be true, I still find my hands grabbing at the illusion of control from time to time.

It's in these moments where I have to remind myself of who God is; of His character and of His heart.

I remind myself that the same God who led the Israelites to the Red Sea and split the sea so they could walk through on dry land is the same God who hears my prayers.

I remind myself that the same God who used evil kings and abhorrent cultures to bring His purposes to fruition can use even my most trying of circumstances to do the same.

I remind myself that the same God who brought three Hebrew children out unscathed from a fiery furnace is the same God who watches over me as I sleep.

I remind myself that He hasn't changed – and that He won't.

When I am rooted in the truth of who God is – I am rooted in a right view of the world and of my circumstances. I am not just focused on dealing with the ramifications of a change – but I see the change as an instrument through which God moves. For my glory and for His good.

Because He is good – I can rest assured knowing His plans for me are good too.

This is the message we have heard from him and proclaim to you, that God is light, and in him is no darkness at all.

1 John 1:5 (ESV)

KICK AROUND QUESTIONS

1. What is your favorite quality of God? Feel free to use the list above or to choose one of your own.

2. What is one quality of God that is hardest for you to grasp and believe? Why?

PRAYER NUDGE

Thank God for who He is. Ask Him to reveal His character to you in ways He never has before. Focus on your favorite quality of Him and tell Him why that means so much to you. Confess to Him that it is hard to believe He is _____. Ask Him to show you in real, tangible ways that He is _____, despite your inability to see it right away. Meditate (meaning read / think about / say over and over again) some of the qualities of God that are particularly relevant to you in this season of change.

DAY 27
GOD'S PLACE

In college, I remember singing the song "Center" by Charlie Hall at a Fellowship of Christian Athletes meeting. We packed as many students as we could into the white clubhouse that sat on the north side of our campus' lake. My friend, Kyle, was leading worship the first time I heard this song – and I remember being struck by the lyrics.

"You hold everything together,
You hold everything together.
Oh, Christ, be the center of our lives,
Be the places we fix our eyes,
Be the center of our lives."

At that point in my life, I'd come to understand God's location as over our lives – meaning, as we covered earlier, He was sovereign (the fancy Christian way of saying He was in control). I'd also heard it said – over and over again – that when it came to dating, God should be at the center of any relationship.

But the center of my life? As a whole? It was kind of a revolutionary concept, despite the fact that I'd been a Christian for over 10 years at that point. I felt like I was somehow missing out by not knowing how God could be at the center of my life. You might say I got a little hung up on the semantics – but I couldn't quite wrap my head around it.

You see, I knew that God was in Heaven, reigning over all the earth.

I also knew that because I'd entered into a relationship with God through the saving work of Jesus, the Holy Spirit dwelt inside me as God made my heart His temple.

I also knew that scripture promised God was with me – never to leave me nor forsake me.

I also knew that God went before me wherever I went – reassuring me that I had nothing to fear.

To recap: God was in Heaven, within me, with me and before me. But I couldn't arrive at a place where I understood Him to be at the center of my life.

What did that even look like? Was I Holy enough – Christian enough – for that to be true in my life?

This is a part of my story I'm a little bit ashamed of – but in the spirit of transparency – I know God wants me to share.

In this particular season of my life – in efforts to make God the center – I got a little bit legalistic. If you're not familiar with the whole concept of legalism, for our purposes, it means trying to earn favor with God by following all of the rules and, essentially, striving to be perfect. (Because we know that we can never follow the rules well enough to earn favor with God, we know we need Jesus. Praise God for Jesus!)

The way this legalism manifested itself in my life was equal parts prideful and shameful. On the weeks before cross country or track meets, I would try and be "extra good."

I wouldn't make out with my boyfriend.

I would be sure to write long, flowery prayers in my prayer journal.

I would read my Bible at least once a day.

I wouldn't curse or listen to any raunchy music.

I would try to be extra polite to my parents on the phone – even if I disagreed with them.

In my head, if I followed all of the rules and washed up the outside to make myself look righteous and holy – God would allow me to run fast and perform well in my race. I operated under the guise of that transactional relationship we talked about a few days ago and thought that if I did _____, for God, He would bless me.

Talk about bad theology, am I right?

In efforts to "center my life" on God – I tried to *do more for Him* instead of *being with Him more*. On the surface, my intentions seemed okay – holy even – but when I looked at them with a deeper honesty, it became clear that I was putting bandages on bullet holes.

In order for God to be at the center of our lives, everything else must truly revolve around His love for us. And that love for us? It should pull everything we think, say, or do into His holy orbit.

Because God is with us, we ought to know better than to think we can trick Him into thinking we're holier than we actually are.

Because His Spirit lives within us, our thoughts, actions and speech ought to reflect the grace that saved our soul.

Because our hearts have been transformed, our outward lives ought to be too. And not just because we want something out of the deal.

When I look at the concept of the Trinity (the belief in one God in three persons: God the Father, God the Son and God the Holy Spirit), I get a glimpse of the accurate position of God in my life.

When I think of God the Father – I think of the King on the throne. I see Him "on high," as the Bible states, seated on the Heavenly Throne, surrounded by Heavenly Hosts. He is exalted (read: praised and worshiped) because He is the one true King and He is worthy of all glory and honor and praise.

It is this image of God that roots me in my belief that God is over my life.

When I think of God the Son (Jesus), I think of God with flesh on. I see God humbling Himself to live as human, to dwell among the people He longed to save. I see His love poured out on the cross, making us right with Himself through His sacrificial death and resurrection.

It is this image of God where I most clearly envision Him right next to me – in the trenches with me, never leaving me.

When I think of God the Holy Spirit, I think of the power that raised Jesus from the dead. I don't necessarily see the Holy Spirit – but I feel it. It's a part of me. It's another piece that will never leave me, but it's because it lives within me.

The Holy Spirit is where I see God within me – dwelling inside my heart and soul.

It is when I focus on the combination of all these locations – the omnipresence of the triune God – that I see my thoughts, speech and actions center on Him. It is through this lens where my life truly revolves around Him.

There is one body and one Spirit—just as you were called to the one hope that belongs to your call— one Lord, one faith, one baptism, one God and Father of all, who is over all and through all and in all.

Ephesians 4:4-6 (ESV)

KICK AROUND QUESTIONS

1. Be honest – what is God's place in your life? Is He truly at the center of it all?

2. Have you ever wrestled with trying to "trick God" into thinking you were something you weren't? Confess it and write about it.

PRAYER NUDGE

Talk with God about your desire (or lack thereof) for Him to be at the center of your life. If you desire Him to be at the center – ask Him to show you ways to make Him the center. Ask Him to show you what to forsake and what to lean into. If you don't desire it – be honest with Him. (He can take it, I promise!) Ask Him to change your heart – to give you a spirit that is willing to be willing – and ask Him to remind you of His great love for you in whatever place you are in.

DAY 28
YOUR IDENTITY

I waited 28 days – 28 whole days! – for you to read this chapter.

Bits of this part of my story are trickled throughout the book (see Day 8) – but so much of who I am today is because of the life-changing transformation God orchestrated through one of the darkest seasons of my life.

To be perfectly blunt: 2016 was simultaneously the absolute best and absolute worst year of my life.

I got married – but I hit rock bottom.

Tyler moved in – but so did an anxiety and panic disorder.

We honeymooned to Charleston – but when I came back to Charlotte, my mind got sicker and sicker.

I invested in counseling – but it wasn't "working" in the way I thought it should.

I turned to the Lord in the midst of my struggle – but I couldn't quite see His hands in any of the despair I was walking through.

I was overjoyed to start this new chapter with my Tyler – but I felt as though I was a prisoner in my own mind.

It sounds dramatic – but I was absolutely miserable.

In the middle of a crippling season of anxiety and panic, I did the only thing I knew to do: Go to God over and over and over again.

I talked a good bit about how God threw me a ladder and helped me climb out of the pit – and by His goodness, *Because I'm His* was born. In the darkest place that seemed absent of any kind of hope or change – God turned my misery into my ministry.

At the root of my bout with anxiety and panic was a warped identity. It was bad theology. It was lies disguised as truth.

For years, I'd given the enemy more than foothold. For years, I'd given him direct access to my soul by allowing him to whisper accusations about who I was and who I would always be in my ear. And because these lies weren't *that* bombastic, I passively accepted them as truth. You see, these accusations were no doubt rooted in the truth of the things I'd done, said, thought and let happen. They were rooted in the reality that I was a sinful human with a heart perpetually bent toward self, fear and the endless desire to control.

Yet, in believing these lies and accepting them as truth – I was making God out to be a liar. It was as if by heeding the hissing condemnation of the enemy, I was putting my stake in the ground and telling God that I no longer believed the things He said about me. By believing things like, "I'll always be the anxious one," or "I am a unique breed of crazy no one could ever understand or fix," I was living in a false identity.

And so, I had to dig to find my true one.

Because I'm His started as a personal Instagram account that overflowed out of a need to remind myself of who I was. I needed to know what my Creator – God – said about me and so I wrote about it and paired it with pretty pictures of women who embodied joy, freedom and peace.

When I made it public, it a little bit took off and suddenly, I realized I wasn't the only one who was hungry to know what God had to say about identity. It's because of this part of my story that there is such an intense passion deep within me for women to know their Biblical identities.

Why? Because it's through a firm and rooted understanding of our Biblical identities – of knowing who we are – that we can face change and transition with brave faces and full hearts. It's because our true, Biblical identity never changes. It doesn't ebb and flow when seasons change or we walk through the unknown. Our identity as a loved daughter of the King is as constant as constant gets.

I long for women to know this. I long for women to know what their Creator, their King and their God has to say about who He intentionally created them to be. I long for them to walk in the true and freeing abundance that is knowing who they are because of Jesus Christ.

Because we are His…
— We are safe (2 Thessalonians 3:3)
— We are cared for (1 Peter 5:7)
— We can rest (Exodus 33:14)
— We are free (Galatians 5:1)
— We can laugh (Proverbs 31:25)
— We have no shame (Isaiah 54:4)
— We have worth (Romans 5:8)
— We are forgiven (1 John 1:9)
— We can hope (Romans 8:24-25)
— We have purpose (Ephesians 2:10)

— We can trust (Psalm 28:7)
— We have joy (1 Peter 1:8)
— We have peace (John 16:33)
— We are whole (James 1:4)
— We are chosen (John 15:16)
— We are delivered (Psalm 32:7)
— We are brave (Psalm 34:4)
— We are not alone (Deuteronomy 31:6)
— We are secure (Hebrews 6:19)
— We are reconciled (Romans 5:10)
— We are redeemed (Isaiah 43:1)
— We are strong (2 Corinthians 12:9-10)
— We have a place (John 14:2)
— We are comforted (2 Corinthians 1:3-4)
— We are made new (2 Corinthians 5:17)
— We are called good (Genesis 1:31)
— We are fully known and fully loved (Jeremiah 1:5)

*So you are no longer a slave, but a son, and if a
son, then an heir through God.*

Galatians 4:7 (ESV)

KICK AROUND QUESTIONS

1. Think of a particularly difficult change you're walking through (or have walked through) and write down some of the ways having a rooted identity in Christ might change the way you walk through it.

2. Circle three identifying qualities from the list above and re-write them with your name. For example, if you pick, "We are brave," write, "Your Name is brave."

PRAYER NUDGE

Talk to God about some of the ways you need to lean into the woman He's intentionally created you to be. Ask Him to remind you of who you are because you are His and ask Him to keep the truth of your identity at the forefront of your mind when you are going through seasons of transition or change. Brainstorm with God on some of the ways you've been allowing your circumstances (good or bad) to define you and replace the lies (again, good and bad lies!) with the truth of who He says you are.

DAY 29
YOUR PLACE

On Day 27, we talked about God's place in our story. We talked about how He is with us, within us and at the center of everything we do. Today I want to help you shift your mind and think about your place – not just in your story, but in His story.

The Bible (Romans 8:17) tells us that because we are God's children, we are an heir (or heiress) of God, joint heirs (or heiresses) with Christ. This means that as we share in Christ's sufferings, so too we will share in His glory in Heaven. The Greek word here is *sugkléronomos*, which literally means a joint heir or participant.

I don't know about you – but I love the distinction of us being participants in Christ's glory. I love the proximity it infers – a closeness, a nearness, a presence.

You see, we can be "co-heirs" from a distance. We can inherit something without ever even speaking with someone – and this happens all of the time in today's world. In fact, I'm sure you know someone who inherited something from the passing of a relative – someone who they may not have even seen in recent history.

But to participate – we need to be near. I cannot truly participate in something if I am not present. Even in the reality of social media and technology making our world smaller and smaller – there are few things we can truly participate in from afar.

To participate means to be present. To be present speaks to a location. And location? It speaks to a place. This verse clearly tells us that – one day – we will share physical proximity with God in Heaven.

And when we get there, we get to participate in God's glory because God has given us a place of righteousness through the saving work of Jesus Christ. Because He took the wrath of God – the wrath we deserved because of our sin – we are made right with God and given a place of virtue with God. Because of the sacrifice Jesus made – we have peace with God. And when God looks at us? He sees the sinless righteousness of Jesus.

But what about our place now?

For now, we live in a broken world where we are tasked with bringing the peace and joy and abundance of His kingdom. It's a big undertaking and it's one we can do only with the guiding help of the Holy Spirit and in community with other believers.

It's in this place where we experience the heartbreak and discomfort of change and transition.

It's in this place where we ache for security and peace and joy.

But Christians often say, "This world is not our home," or, "We're just passing through." These phrases capture the Biblical truth that we were not made for this world, but instead, we are citizens of Heaven (Philippians 3:20). Yet often times, Christians (myself, at one time, included) fall prey to the belief that we can only fully experience His peace and joy and goodness when we get to Heaven. We believe that because we live in a fallen world, we only get glimpses of His goodness and don't get to truly experience any of it fully.

I am not sure about the theological soundness of what I am about to say – so take this with a grain of salt and do some research if it doesn't sit well with you – but I don't think that's what God wants for us. I don't think He teases out His goodness like an appetizing preview on this side of Heaven, only to truly fulfill it when we breathe our last breath on this earth. I don't think He came to give us abundant life (John 10:10), but only to fully give it to us in Heaven.

I believe – with all of my heart – that we can experience the fullness of that abundant life in the here and now.

I believe this because of the proximity to God we have now – because of the in dwelling Holy Spirit.

I believe this because of the place of righteousness Jesus gives us.

I believe this because God looks at us and sees a blameless daughter who He longs to use for His glory.

And that full, abundant life? I believe we can live in a place with it now, even when everything changes. I believe it's our place with God – near to Him, next to Him and right with Him – that enables us to thrive in the midst of life's rocky transitions.

Do you?

But God, being rich in mercy, because of the great love with which he loved us, even when we were dead in our trespasses, made us alive together with Christ—by grace you have been saved— and raised us up with him and seated us with him in the heavenly places in Christ Jesus, so that in the coming ages he might show the immeasurable riches of his grace in kindness toward us in Christ Jesus.

Ephesians 2:4-7 (ESV)

KICK AROUND QUESTIONS

1.   Write 2-3 sentences about your current place in life. Are you in a place of peace? A place of despair? A place of joy? A place of anxiety? A place of growing? A place of seeking?

2.   Read Ephesians 2:4-7 again and reflect on how that truth may impact whatever place you are currently in.

PRAYER NUDGE

Praise God for His rich mercy and great love. Thank Him for making us alive together with Christ – for granting us as co-heirs, as participants in His glory. Ask Him to remind you of the right standing we have with Him because of Jesus and to show you how you can live in full abundance now – on this side of eternity.

DAY 30
YOUR FUTURE

L et's talk about what I believe is certain: Death will come for us all. It doesn't discriminate. And none of us make it out alive.

But here's what I also believe with just as much certainty: When I breathe my last breath on this earth, I will breathe my first breath in Heaven. I believe with full conviction that the years I will live in this world – whether it's 29 or 129 – will be just a small blip on the radar of eternity. I believe whole heartedly in the truth of John 3:16 – that because I have a saving relationship with Jesus, I will not truly die, but have everlasting, eternal life with God in Heaven.

I love how the Message version words and confirms this for me in the book of Ephesians. In this book, Paul is writing to the church at Ephesus and, in so many words, he is describing how the truth of the Gospel should affect our everyday lives. In chapter 1, verses 11 through 14, Paul writes:

> It's in Christ that we find out who we are and what we are living for. Long before we first heard of Christ and got our hopes up, he had his eye on us, had designs on us for glorious living, part of the overall purpose he is working out in everything and everyone.

It's in Christ that you, once you heard the truth and believed it (this Message of your salvation), found yourselves home free—signed, sealed, and delivered by the Holy Spirit. This signet from God is the first installment on what's coming, a reminder that we'll get everything God has planned for us, a praising and glorious life.
(Ephesians 1:11-14 [MSG])

The New American Standard version calls the Holy Spirit the "down payment" of our inheritance, in essence saying, that His dwelling within us now is an "advance payment" and that the rest of it will surely be given to us. The "praising and glorious" life is a promise God has planned for us in eternity. We will "cash in" on that promise when we cross the finish line of this life and enter into the glory of the next.

As Christians, we can believe this and rest in this with complete and utter certainty. As Christians, we have ultimate security because – despite change and transition and uncertainty and upheaval – we know how the story ends.

My sweet Tyler likes to remind me of this truth when I catch myself leaning into anxiety or worry. With such grace, gentleness and conviction, he reminds me, "Sweetheart, remember: It's never not okay."

And even when it's hard to hear or believe, even when whatever I am flustered about seems so big and so worthy of a freakout – I know he's right.

As Christians, in spite of a life that's filled with shifting circumstances and unexpected curve balls, it's never not okay. Not even for a second.

In Jesus, our future is secure. No matter what change – good, bad, or ugly – we face on this side of eternity, our future in Heaven is a sure thing. Our future, our being "home free" is signed, sealed and delivered – and there's nothing we could ever experience on this earth that could undo or change that. This – this simple, yet sometimes understated truth – changes how we face everything.

In him you also, when you heard the word of truth, the gospel of your salvation, and believed in him, were sealed with the promised Holy Spirit, who is the guarantee of our inheritance until we acquire possession of it, to the praise of his glory.

Ephesians 1:13-14 (ESV)

KICK AROUND QUESTIONS

1.   What are some of your hopes for your future?

2.   How does a secure future in Christ change the way you live now? How does it change the way you might face certain changes or major life transitions?

PRAYER NUDGE

Ask God for a perspective change - for an eternal outlook on life. Ask Him to change the way you view change - for a perspective that is rooted in the secure certainty of your future in eternity with Him - not in your circumstances on this earth. Praise Him for a sealed future, for an eternal home in Heaven.

AFTERWORD

My greatest hope for this book is simple: To open your eyes to the reality that you can thrive in the midst of life's most challenging changes.

Not because you are strong and self-sufficient.

Not because you aren't emotional and don't get attached to things, people or places.

Not because you stuff your feelings or don't talk about your struggles.

Not because you are easygoing or carefree or chill.

No.

My hope is that over the past 30-days (or however many days it took you to get through my ramblings), you learned that completely depending on Jesus is the only way to have a healthy relationship with change.

My hope is that as you read these last few paragraphs – you have a new lease on life through a new perspective that points you to Jesus. I pray that in my obedience to write this devotional and put my brokenness on display for all who read to see, God has spoken to you in a way that invites you to trust Him more than you did when you started.

Reading this book isn't going to make change easier for you. I'm sure you know this – but just in case you don't – this book didn't just cure you of being reluctant to jump up and down when change comes your way. But what I hope this book did is walk you through what it looks like to lean into God in the midst of the chaos; to hide yourself in the consistency of His goodness when things go awry.

Change is hard. And if I'm honest, I believe certain types of changes just always will be.

But because of God – we get to have joy even when change comes knocking. We get to have peace even when we desire change more than we can express. We get to rest in the security of our future even when change threatens everything we know.

Because of God, we can thrive and not just survive when everything changes.

And sister, I pray you do just that as you close the final page of this book.

You are His,

Diana

ABOUT THE AUTHOR

Diana Carter is a writer and teacher enamored by the vision of a generation of women boldly embracing their Biblical identities. She spends her weeks as a Communications Director at Forest Hill Church in Charlotte, NC where she lives with her husband, Tyler. Diana founded *Because I'm His*, an online community committed to equipping women in their true identities, in 2016.

In between all of the serious stuff, you can usually find her with Tyler: shamelessly binge-watching Bravo! or brewery hopping with friends.

You can follow *Because I'm His* on Instagram @becauseimhis or visit www.becauseimhis.com.

Made in the USA
San Bernardino, CA
30 August 2018